Great Kids' Rooms

Great Kids' Rooms

Decorating Ideas for All Their Years at Home

Carol Scheffler

Sterling Publishing Co., Inc. New York
A Sterling / Chapelle Book

Chapelle, Ltd.:

owner: Jo Packham

editor: Caroll Shreeve

art director/designer: Karla Haberstich

staff: Areta Bingham, Kass Burchett,
Ray Cornia, Jill Dahlberg, Marilyn Goff,
Holly Hollingsworth, Susan Jorgensen,
Barbara Milburn, Karmen Quinney,
Cindy Stoeckl, Kim Taylor,
Sara Toliver, Desirée Wybrow

Library of Congress Cataloging-in-Publication Data

Scheffler, Carol
    Great kids' rooms : decorating ideas for all their years at
       home / Carol Scheffler.
       p. cm.
    Includes index.
    ISBN 0-8069-8285-3
    1. Children's rooms. 2 Interior decoration. I. Title.

    NK2117.C4 S33 2002
    747.7'7--dc21

                  2002066870

10 9 8 7 6 5 4 3 2 1
Published by Sterling Publishing Co., Inc.
387 Park Avenue South, New York, NY 10016
©2002 by Carol Scheffler
Distributed in Canada by Sterling Publishing
c/o Canadian Manda Group, One Atlantic Avenue, Suite 105
Toronto, Ontario, Canada M6K 3E7
Distributed in Great Britain and Europe by Chrysalis Books
64 Brewery Road, London N7 9NT, England
Distributed in Australia by Capricorn Link (Australia) Pty. Ltd.
P.O. Box 704, Windsor, NSW 2756, Australia
Printed in China
All Rights Reserved

Sterling ISBN 0-8069-8285-3

If you have any questions or comments, please contact:

Chapelle, Ltd., Inc.
P.O. Box 9252
Ogden, UT 84409

(801) 621-2777
Fax (801) 621-2788

e-mail: chapelle@chapelleltd.com
website: www.chapelleltd.com

Getting Started

Great kids' rooms begin with who your great kids are and what interests them. That's your design starting point as decorating parents.

Kids spend so much of their young lives in their rooms. There they learn to walk, build a blanket fort, dress for their first day of school, cry over a broken heart, cram for finals, and one day, learn to say goodbye. Make their rooms special. A great kid's room is easier to conceive and create, and less expensive than you may think.

Great Kids' Rooms is a style guide for big ideas, focal-point approaches, and design details to make a decorating success of your kid's room. Learn how to "grow" a room with your child, using transformations from nursery to teen, with just a few changes. This book helps you plan rooms that meet your children's changing growth needs and interests.

The focus is on key concerns of decorating a child's room: safety; nursery needs; as well as floor, wall, window, lighting, storage, furniture, and decorative options. Consider the different ways rooms need to function for play, work, entertaining, and sleep.

A style book on decorating must inspire! This one does. Get ideas from our photographs and tips on inventive, fresh, and functional rooms.

Carol Scheffler

Did you know?

Kids get excited when they hear their bedroom's going to get a make-over. They have dreams of how they want it to look, what they'll be able to do there, and they imagine how much fun it will be to see their new room. Involve their ideas and their energy.

How to Use This Book

Table of Contents

Kids are each so unique in their personalities, energy levels, interests, and temperaments. To decorate rooms for them successfully, address their personal needs. When children share space, or a new baby means a nursery must be created again, family priorities change. Finances ebb and flow. Enjoy decorating flexibly.

Family Harmony Room by Room

Parents with any age of children are living a day-to-day adventure. Decorating kids' rooms to make them great is part of the fun of parenting. Involving kids in the process makes decorating a positive bonding experience. This is an opportunity to talk about what really matters to them and to take the details of those special conversations into consideration for selecting a theme and making it happen.

For a child above the infant stage, do not underestimate the importance of their input as a first step to any decorating adventure. Keen observation of even a toddler's preferences for textures, colors, shapes, sizes, and objects is vital information for the people in charge of creating a special bedroom or play space. A room with style is a room with personality. It should reflect the personality of the child who lives there, as well as the taste of the parents who are guiding the growing up process. The older the child, the more actively they can participate in every step of the decorating of their room. Take advantage of your children's creative

imaginations. Restrain your desire as a parent to impose your childhood dream room on your little ones. Older kids will be more forthright in saying what they want. Help children of any age to make practical as well as wishful choices for their living space. Teach them that the success of any project depends upon the supporting details, not how much you spend.

Great Kids' Rooms will help you bring a personal touch to your children's rooms. After all, your personal touch is apparent in every aspect of their lives—it should certainly be present in their bedrooms and play spaces!

What an exciting time in your life. What a fulfilling project you are about to embark on.

Your child's room has a skeleton. The walls, windows, floors, doors, and ceilings are the bones of the space. Each must be considered for safety, lighting, living, play, storage needs, and decorating style. Think and plan before you spend.

architectural elements

Before You Begin Decorating

Once you have appraised your child's needs, or those of children who will share a space, it is time to look at the architectural elements of the room. With age of the child, safety, comfort, and expenditure limits in mind, carefully consider each structural element of the space as it exists now. What must be done to the floor: nonskid paint for a rumpus room, soft carpet for quiet nursery, roll-up rugs for building with blocks or dancing?

Are there so many doors and windows that traffic patterns are awkward or built-ins need to be created? Can a closet be sacrificed to make a study area? Would shelves around the ceiling solve a collector's nightmare? How easy can keeping order be made for your child's personality and life-style?

Answering these sorts of questions will open your mind to how to take advantage of the creative ideas in this book.

With both short- and long-range plans clear, select a theme, an inspirational focal point, a color palette, and decide if floors, ceilings, or walls are your starting point. Purchase paint for the entire project, so colors will match throughout with enough left for touch-ups.

Flooring Options

There is no other surface in your child's room that will get used harder and withstand more abuse than the floor. Cost, comfort, durability, ease of maintenance, ease of installation, and style will all play a part in your floor-treatment decision. Where a bath adjoins, transition carefully.

Wood

The plus side of hardwood floors is that they are easy to maintain. Vacuuming and an occasional dust-mopping removes dirt and dust. For a child with allergies where dust can be a real problem, wood floors are a particularly good choice. The drawbacks to consider are that oftentimes installation is a process best left to experts; adding hardwood floors can be expensive; and wood is an unforgiving surface to a toddler learning to walk. However, it is an ideal firm surface to play on with trains, building blocks, games, and puzzles. If the finish on existing wood floors is unacceptable as they are, and the cost to refinish is prohibitive, they can be painted with specially formulated floor enamels in neutral or bright colors and sealed.

Alternative Flooring

Resilient and laminate floorings offer beauty in a wider variety of color and pattern at a lower cost.

wood floor

Hardwood, laminate, painted, and resilient floors are ideal for moving furniture on rollers. Use acrylic carpet protectors if you select otherwise.

skid pad

Paint A painted wood or concrete floor in one color can make a dramatic statement, or use several colors and theme images such as stars, flowers, borders, and pretend roads. Prepare and prime according to paint directions for the surface you are covering. Take the advice of your paint store expert.

Carpeting Have experts install wall-to-wall carpeting. It comes in limitless colors, patterns, and materials. Wool is the most expensive, but offers the most durability. It is naturally fire-resistant. If your crawling child is allergic to wool, an acrylic fiber is best. Synthetic carpeting is less expensive, but doesn't feel as nice. Wool/synthetic blends are good for cost savings and durability. Purchase stain-resistant carpeting or treat it yourself. Dark colors and patterns hide stains. Buy the best carpet padding thickness and quality you can afford for long-term wear, maximum cushion comfort, and superior soundproofing in the room and those adjacent to it.

The nursery is a gentle place for a newborn's sleeping times, often at hours that are opposite those of the rest of the family. Take into account the sleeping needs of others in surrounding rooms and on floors below. It will be helpful to everyone else's rest if the rocker area has a well-padded carpet or area rug.

Introduction — Flooring Options

11

Floors Active kids need rugged and safe floor treatments in their play areas. The more children who will play in a given space, the more likely the need for durable material solutions. If you are fortunate enough to have a play area in the bedroom for trikes, race car tracks, train sets, and roller skates, then consider paint treatments for wood. Even bright colors and stenciled designs can be effectively sealed with polyurethane for long-term wear, so the space is always fun. Paint roads, parking lots, airstrips, and bridges on the floor. Make playtime a delightful experience for groups of children or for one who prefers to play alone with cars and blocks.

2-7 years old

Paint theme designs that match room accents for a fresh treatment on an old floor. You may want to paint only a border around the carpeted center of the room. Purchase stencils or make your own.

For a textured "flagstone" floor, tear brown paper bags into rock shapes, crush into découpage medium or glue/water mixture (creamy not watery) and adhere to the floor, overlapping the edges. Dry, then seal with two coats polyurethane.

15-college age

Rugs Consider the activity level and interests of your children when selecting rugs for their rooms. Expensive wall-to-wall carpet may be easily stained or irreparably harmed by the painter, bug collector, pizza- or pet-loving kid's activities. Temporary solutions that get a room through the stages of a child's needs by age can be made in throw or area rugs. Such options include: hooked and shag area rugs, painted floorcloths, painted vinyl area rugs, and stitched-together carpet sample squares. If only the visual effect of a rug is needed, paint a border or a simple to elaborate pattern in your theme directly on the floor. When the need arises, simply cover with carpet or sand and repaint.

infant

8-14 years old

15-college age

Back a lighter-weight rug with nonskid strips. It can be rolled out of the way for toys and games.

Wool felt and pile are excellent soft and quiet rug choices for infant rooms.

Leather rugs are hardy surfaces for teen to adult rooms.

Walls and Windows

Choosing your child's wall covering is the decorating choice that will cover the most square footage of the room and will have the most transforming impact. There are three types of covering to consider: wallpaper, paint, and fabric. You may combine them. Windows, as important wall and light elements, must also be considered at this decorating stage.

Wallpaper

There is an established architectural appearance to wallpaper. It is available in thousands of prints, colors, and styles. Narrow your choices of color, theme, and scale to help select the best wall covering. Some designers lay down hard-and-fast rules such as: "Avoid trendy characters in wall coverings," or "In a small room use a smaller print paper," or "Pick a gender-neutral paper that can work for any child." It is helpful to consider family common-sense suggestions, then go buy whatever you and your child love. Whether or not you hire someone to hang your paper, there is cost involved in materials and perhaps labor. Think long-term, even though you can change the

paper. Vinyl paper washes clean with more ease than regular wallpaper. Many papers come with coordinating borders that can be added above a chair rail, at the top of the wall where it meets the ceiling, or on the ceiling edge where it meets the wall. Borders can add architectural interest in a room that lacks wood detail. Borders can be used by themselves over a painted wall. Many wallpapers come with coordinating fabric that can be sewn into bedding and window treatments to pull together a coordinated bedroom look.

Another option is to determine one or two walls that can be papered and then paint the others. To determine how much paper you will need, provide the height and width room

Stripes and plaid are ideal pattern choices for parents who hang their own paper. Match each new strip to the previous one at the design. If papering an older home where walls have settled, be subtle with color and contrast to diminish problem areas.

measurements, minus the window and door areas, to your wallpaper store. The number of rolls needed based on the dimensions, the repeat of design, and the width of paper will be calculated. Order extra paper to repair a damaged wall later.

Paint To achieve the biggest impact in the room for the least amount of money, paint is ideal. Buy the best paint you can afford for better coverage and durability. Use latex as opposed to oil-based paint. Its advantages are soap-and-water cleanup, less fumes, quicker drying time, and it has the coverage and durability of oil-based paint. Paints are available in a variety of colors or can be custom colored to match a fabric or floor covering. Painting a room does not require a professional. Take a swatch to the paint store and provide the room dimensions and condition of what you are covering. They calculate how much you need by the coats necessary for rich color without bleed-through.

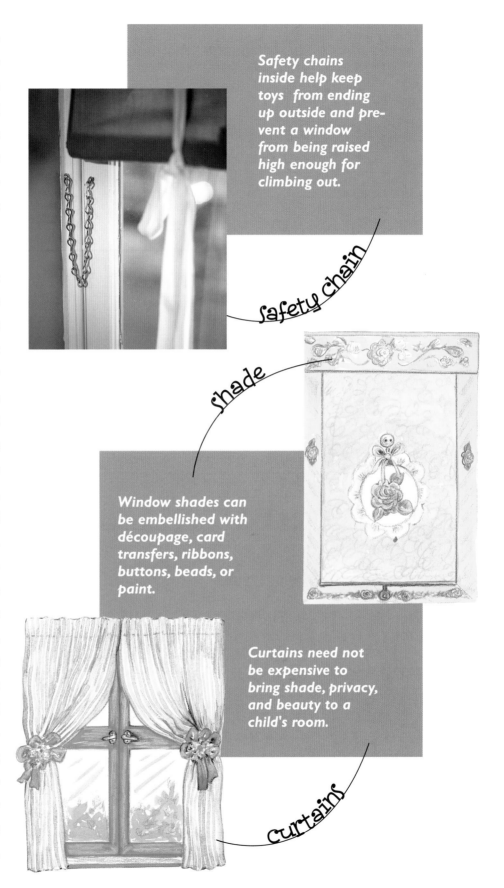

Safety chains inside help keep toys from ending up outside and prevent a window from being raised high enough for climbing out.

safety chain

shade

Window shades can be embellished with découpage, card transfers, ribbons, buttons, beads, or paint.

Curtains need not be expensive to bring shade, privacy, and beauty to a child's room.

curtains

Lighting There are three types of lighting beyond natural light: ambient (overall), task (illuminate targeted areas for specific activities), and accent (decorative fixtures that highlight small areas or groups of objects). Your rooms will require all three types of lighting.

Small children need a variety of lighting options. Track, recessed, or central ceiling fixtures provide excellent ambient lighting. If properly installed and maintained, they offer no safety concerns. Wall fixtures and free-standing lamps are excellent sources of task lighting, in areas where coloring, games, reading, and hobbies take place. Add a dimmer switch to any wall-controlled light for flexibility and to act as a night-light, easing the disturbance of parents checking on little ones.

lighting options

Bedside lighting with theme lamps is easy and fun. Task lighting for study, handwork, and hobbies is of higher intensity and available in eye-saving options with flexible arms.

Where balls are bounced, recessed canister lighting is an ideal choice. It's great for safety in stairwells, too.

Track or strip lighting allows for moving each lamp and directing it to illuminate a specific area.

track lighting

Storage Kids love to accumulate stuff! Changes of seasons and a variety of activities produce enough clothes to fill closets and dresser drawers. Birthday and holiday gifts pile up. Collections of personal treasures should be displayed with pride. The trick to creating a great kid's space is to organize, store, and display all that stuff.

Clothes last longer when stored properly. A well-designed closet ideally has two hanging rods of varying heights. Hang one the child can reach with ease for selecting and hanging up daily clothing. A second higher rod is suitable for storing off-season and rarely worn items. Storage drawers can be built-ins under a bed, in a closet, or in a wall. Traditionally they are available in dresser and bureau furniture. Be certain that all furniture you purchase conforms to the Consumer Product Safety Commission. (Check the label.)

The older and more active your child, the more space you will need in your plan. Soccer uniforms, ballet and workout gear, camp clothing and swimwear, are all among the items beyond daily school and play clothes that require storage space. Pegs and wall knobs can store bulky items out in the open for easy access and decorative interest. Pull-out shelves and pull-down bins offer storage options for sports equip-

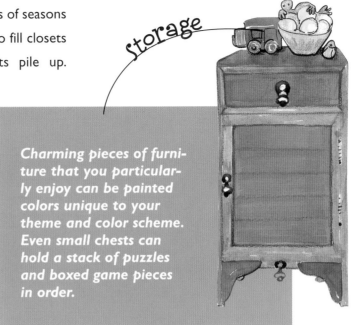

Storage

Charming pieces of furniture that you particularly enjoy can be painted colors unique to your theme and color scheme. Even small chests can hold a stack of puzzles and boxed game pieces in order.

ment, computer components, hats, and odd-shaped toys.

Keep everything accessible and easy to put away. Organize by "stations" near activity areas where the items will be used: puzzles near a play table, crayons by the paper, and swim goggles next to earplugs.

Storage

Use every space available for storage—pull-out drawers under bunks and window seats, open shelves, shelves with clear bins or baskets labeled for their contents.

17

Decorative Accents Quilt blocks, button collections, greeting and playing cards are uniquely personal items that can be matted and framed for display in children's rooms. Effective in rooms with an obvious theme, they need not be expensive investments. Thrift shops, yard sales, calendars, and picture books offer a wealth of materials to use for framed art. Baby's christening gown, a set of baseball trading cards, and the child's own art, perhaps from various ages, are accent possibilities.

Image on glass

1. Scan and copy selected image onto decal paper using color copier from a copy center, even if black and white. Follow manufacturer's instructions.

2. Soak decal paper in warm water for one minute, and transfer onto front of glass. Follow manufacturer's instructions.

3. Squeegee out air bubbles. Let dry for 24 hours.

4. Apply clear matte water-based varnish. Follow manufacturer's instructions.

Crackled Window Frame

1. Paint frame with base color. This is color that will show through cracks. It may take more than one coat to cover. Let dry

2. Using long sweeping strokes, apply crackle medium. Follow manufacturer's instructions. A thin coat will produce fine cracks, a thick coat will produce large cracks. Let dry 1–4 hours.
Note: Crackle medium can also be sponged on.

3. Apply top coat of paint. Do not overlap strokes of paint. As top coat dries, cracks will appear. Let dry completely.

Note: Antiquing medium can also be applied for vintage look if desired.

Project:
Vintage Window

Acrylic paints –
     antique white, green

Color copier

Crackle medium

Decal paper

Image

Paintbrushes

Rubber squeegee

Scissors

Warm water

Water-based varnish – matte

Window with panes

From infant to toddler, the smallest kids inspire special spaces. It's a joy to create cozy, happy bedrooms that stimulate growing minds and fingers. Concoct tactile and visual delights for girl or boy from carefully selected details. Each new baby can use such a nursery space because with a change or two, it's a room for either boy or girl. Comfortable spreads and theme toys invite snuggling nap times and prepare for an irresistible rest and play space.

Up I go . . . on tippy toe . . . so I am tall . . . to reach it all!

— unknown

Celebrate with Each New Baby

An imaginative blend of vintage and new brings a shabby-chic style to the baby's room. This delightful pink pedal car sets the transportation theme for a girl. Later, as a second baby arrives, the room can be easily transformed into a boy's nursery if necessary. Retro toys join a decorative-only crib. A newer crib that meets today's safety standards is placed elsewhere in the room for the baby.

Simple old and worn furnishings that are gaining new appreciation are key to shabby-chic style decorating. White-on-white, pale pink, light blue, and soft yellow wrap the look of long ago and deliver it in today's sophistication, via perfect little accents. From chrome to painted metal crib, old is new again in the nursery.

In the early months of the first year, a crib, changing table, and rocking chair see most of the action for infants. As the first birthday draws near, toddlers not only climb out of their beds, and into and on top of their toys, they also cuddle into snugly places to pretend-read their storybooks to their favorite stuffed animals. Chairs and footstools that make climbing up on tippy toe a safe activity need to be child-sized and untippable. Nubby upholstery fabrics invite the short-attention-span set to cuddle awhile with books and toys.

decorative hooks

Scene-stealing storage solutions can be made from découpaged metal buckets. Simple wooden plaques decorated with practical hooks store items in the open. A charming hand-stamped door sign announces nap-time.

Little Girl Baby's room ought to evoke almost as many "ooh's and ah's" as the infant does. The shabby-chic-style transportation theme includes charming prints of vintage vehicles découpaged onto a series of wooden squares.

Where storage is a challenge, sturdy hooks (above) display shower-gift outfits, bibs, booties, and keep pacifiers, rattles, and teething rings in reach of crib and changing table. Moving a baby boy into this space means hanging his clothing and gift items to change the signature of the room to "boy" without further expense.

1. Cut decorative paper into 3" squares. (Larger pieces are difficult to place and prone to air bubbles.)

2. Using foam brush and working on small area, apply découpage medium to bucket. Place paper square onto glued area. Press out any air bubbles. Apply additional coat of découpage medium on paper. Repeat, covering entire bucket. Let dry overnight.

3. In well-ventilated area, spray bucket with several coats of acrylic spray to further protect découpaged surface.

4. Adhere upholstery trim to outside of bucket with craft glue.

Candy wrappers
Children's art
Children's book illustrations
Colorcopied fabric
Colorcopied photographs
Greeting cards
Maps
Paper leaves
Scrapbook paper
Sheet music
Stamps
Stickers
Wallpaper
Wrapping paper

Project:
Toy Bucket

materials

Acrylic spray

Craft glue

Decorative papers

Découpage medium

Foam brush

Galvanized metal bucket

Scissors

Upholstery trim

Cover the Box

1. Cut wallpaper strip 1" longer than diameter of box and 2" taller than height of box.

2. Make 1" fringe-like cuts along top and bottom of strip, approximately 1" apart.

3. Using foam brush, apply adhesive to wrong side of wallpaper strip.

4. Center box onto sticky side of strip between fringed edges. Roll box along strip so that it adheres. There should be 1" overlap where ends meet. Press out any air bubbles.

5. Fold fringe over into inside of box and down onto bottom of box.

Cover the Lid

1. Cut wallpaper strip 1" longer than diameter of box lid and 1" taller than height of lid.

2. Cut wallpaper circle diameter of top of lid.

3. Make ½" fringe-like cuts along top and bottom of strip approximately ¾" apart.

4. Apply adhesive to wrong side of strip.

5. Center lid edge on strip and roll lid along strip so that it adheres. There should be 1" overlap.

6. Fold fringe over into lid and down on top of lid.

7. Apply adhesive to wrong side of wallpaper circle.

8. Place circle of paper on top of lid and press out any air bubbles.

Project: Cover a Band Box

Chipboard band box

Foam brush

Scissors

Wallpaper

Wallpaper adhesive

Vintage chenille welcomes baby's exploring fingers and delicate skin on bedspreads, pillow shams, stuffed toys, and furniture.

Adorable "designer" machine-washable burp cloths, (with toy car designs at left), were made by stitching soft embossed-velvet fabric squares to hand-dyed cloth diapers. Bolster-style pillows, usually associated with "grown-up" decorating were made from soft washable velvets and satins to decorate baby's bed and double as bumpers for headboard, footboard, and crib side cushions.

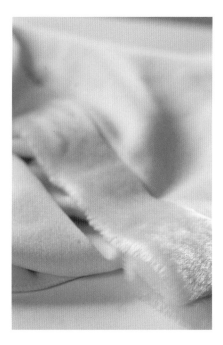

Layette details in edgings, linings, and backings feature secure stitching, impossible to unravel into baby's fingers or mouth. Soft says it all for warmth and comfort.

Decorative as well as practical room accents, these painted wooden hangers with tiny découpaged cutouts are perfect to display sleepers and robes with tiny ribbons and ties.

Decorate walls, shutters, and "clotheslines" of ribbon cord with frequently worn clothing or those that simply look lovely.

initial hooks

Baby's initials cut from wood, fitted with knobs or pegs, then painted, become early learning tools as well as practical hooks.

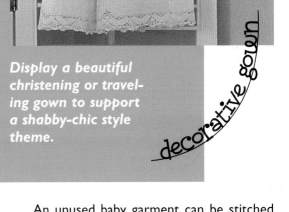

decorative gown

Display a beautiful christening or traveling gown to support a shabby-chic style theme.

An unused baby garment can be stitched closed at the hemline and "pinned" up with style and function. Unbutton it for clean diapers, extra socks, or tiny T-shirts.

Special Occasions

Babies are reason enough to celebrate, but decorate their rooms for holidays, their christenings, and birthdays, too. Stick to your color scheme in the eclectic details for all holiday decorating.

christmas

Even before babies can pull ornaments off the tree, they love to watch the sparkling lights. Create a tree that is added to every year.

valentine

Hearts happening in surprising places make for valentine fun. Whipstitch a row of heart beads to a window shade or make a stuffed-heart flower pocket for wall or window.

For the baby dear to your heart, decorate with valentine pillow accents in pink and rose floral patterns with ruffles and red and white cording.

Baby's first birthday gets a cake in this hat box decorated to look like a frosted treat. Add baby's name, date he first crawled, and his first word. Archive first-year keepsakes inside.

1st birthday

First birthday gifts of red boots and soft toy soccer balls are boyish touches, along with a tiny wooden train that can be handled by a toddler and be the mainstay of a transportation theme.

Little Boy Such a minimal and inexpensive change in what was a girl's room says "boy" now! The basic room elements invested in, if selected carefully, can suffice for all the babies to come. Since most vintage cribs are not safe for baby, and will be decorative theme-setters only, decorate with fun spreads and toys.

Even soft bears (at left) could use a good pillow fresh from the dryer to lean against, especially if they take trips into the washer and dryer themselves. Washable toys and stuffed animals are a must in the little one's environment.

It wouldn't be a shabby-chic-style nursery if comfy details didn't include touches of lace, terry, chenille, ribbons, and huggable stuffed toys. Infants are sensitive to sweet-smelling linens and cotton blankets, just as adults are.

Do not buy or stitch any fabric or bead details on toys or pillows that can be pulled off. If such items arrive as gifts, hang them high and safely out of reach.

Gifts from loved ones almost always duplicate each other, so use the duplicates to prepare at least two portable bags or baskets with blankets, pillows for propping and rest, burp cloths, diapers, and changing supplies. Then spontaneous little trips will be easier even when baby will be needing a nap or a diaper change in a place where everything

A new pillow idea is one that might incorporate using pillows that are traditionally considered "adult" pillows. A second idea might be to take a ready-made pillow case and add lace trim.

pillow

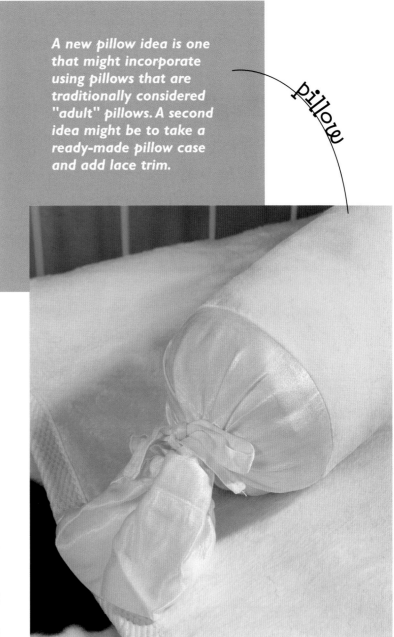

required for comfort won't be available. Two "tiny traveler" bags are best because there will always be a clean one ready to go, even if baby just went on a morning trip requiring a change with one bag, and after a nap, need for a second little journey arises. Being prepared might well include tucking in an ample bath blanket, when all clothing is soaked through in an "accident." Be it the traveling layette or nursery, half the battle of being a stress-free parent of a happy baby is being prepared to comfort.

Chalkboard and magnetic paint make creating scribbling or stick-to-it surfaces fun. Paint walls or furniture tops; add too-fat-to-swallow chalk or magnets.

Surprising Details

The whimsical birdhouse with its honey-dipper perch has a storybook roof and storytelling designs découpaged from the book's torn-out pages.

Toddler-high knobs on a framed and decorated wall area (at left) help even little tots learn that there's a place for everything and that they can help keep order.

Attract little bare toes to a feel-good play area with a fuzzy floor rug to wiggle them in. Group play items in small boxes (under table) for "just enough" blocks to make pick-up-toys time less intimidating for young children.

Engraved Accessories

It's amazing how early toddlers begin to recognize their letters and numbers. Making practical and decorative items into learning tools can't start too early. Make language learning fun for your child with permanent labels on hand-held or "step-up" items that help your child touch letters and learn the sounds of his or her own name. Stamp or emboss them yourself. The picture pocket (above right) is made of felt with a transfer from a vintage card. Fill it with lively alphabet cards and spell out baby's, family, and pet names for learning fun.

This step stool has been stamped with a child's favorite phrase.

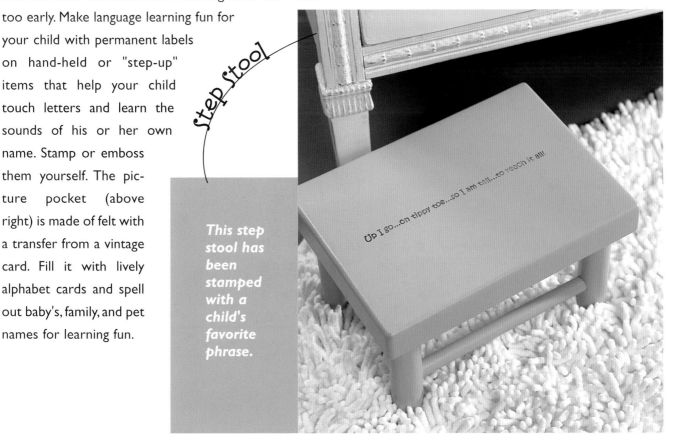

step stool

Up I go...on tippy toe...so I am tall...to reach it all!

Select a sturdy infant bed with side rails that can be lowered or removed and one that is large enough for a two-year-old. Consider a simple, sturdy design that harmonizes well with the other furniture.

Keep the palette neutral. Use easily altered accents: curtains, bed and table skirts, rocker cushions, and table groupings to "grow" the room with the child. How sweet your infant's room will be depends upon your taste. Wall treatments can be faux textures, elaborate stencil, or mural effects in lighthearted themes.

Nursery rhymes and storybook characters make delightful themes for nurseries. Themes can expand as stuffed animal characters and collectibles from the child's favorite told-to and read-aloud stories take up residence. Raggedy Ann, Andy, Peter Rabbit, and any number of bears and bunnies may also come as gifts.

Now, don't get into mischief.
Peter Rabbit — Beatrix Potter

Storybook Tales

The airy, sweet appearance of a nursery is achieved through the minimal use of bright color. White lends an assurance of freshness to baby's new surroundings. A carpeted area is essential near the crib to quietly check on your sleeping infant and for that soft restful atmosphere you want to create.

These wooden picture frames have been painted with pastel colors and the cards received at the baby shower were framed until favorite photography can be added.

Storybook Nurseries

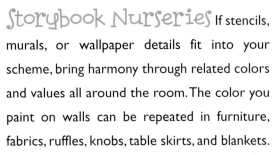

If stencils, murals, or wallpaper details fit into your scheme, bring harmony through related colors and values all around the room. The color you paint on walls can be repeated in furniture, fabrics, ruffles, knobs, table skirts, and blankets.

Think comfort, safety, and quiet in all elements—no groaning doors, squeaky hinges, or glaring lights.

Create interest in a baby's room with rhythms of small focal points to support the main theme. Carry the eye upward with high tiebacks on curtains and little baby-sized items that have interesting details on wall-mounted shelves. Court nurseries had symbolic design elements: ceiling cornices, ruffles on high rods, and outrageously tall toys that predicted baby would grow up to be especially accomplished. The frog at tea (below) is no doubt a prince in disguise for the little princess. Teatime for toys is a focal display, repeated in changing scale.

From early times, the royal treatment for the princess of the realm was a breezy swag swooped from ceiling to puddled folds on the floor. Light organza, netting, or lace can be festooned with ribbons tied to wall knobs and cornice hooks.

swag

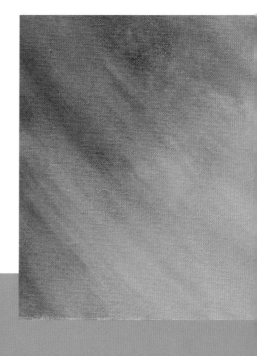

Faux-painted water, sky, and cloud textures make an infant's room heavenly. Sponge and rag blends of three related soft colors can include the furniture—and the ceiling—baby's main view!

wall painting

Paint the wall with a selected "background" color. Enlarged portions of a theme-related picture (right) can then be transferred onto the background and painted, like a coloring book.

Changing tables need side rails. Handy shelves above or below assure you'll not leave baby unattended even for a split second. Add a changing pad to an antique dry sink as another charming option.

Sponge- or stipple-paint background walls, stencil or freehand-draw nursery-theme murals, like the cow jumping over the moon or an underground warren where bunnies eat porridge.

1. Using foam brush, paint shade with pale pink.

2. Using sea sponge, lightly apply darker pink over shade. Let dry completely.

3. Make color copies of illustrations from vintage storybook, reducing or enlarging as necessary.

4. Cut out illustrations and place with removable tape onto shade until you achieve a pleasing arrangement.

5. Remove tape from each cutout. Using foam brush, coat back with découpage medium, then adhere to shade.

6. Cover each cutout with découpage medium. Let dry. Cover entire shade with extra coat of medium. Let dry completely.

7. Adhere coordinating trims onto top and bottom of shade with craft glue. Make certain trimmed ends are in back where shade overlaps. Hold trim in place with clothespins until completely dry.

Project: Découpaged Lamp Shade

Acrylic paint – pink, two shades that are very close

Clothespins

Color copier

Coordinating trims – three

Craft glue

Découpage medium – high-gloss finish

Foam brushes

Lamp shade

Scissors

Sea sponge

Removable tape

Vintage storybook

Frames of all sizes, widths, and shapes are easy to find or make. Leave frame plain or glue on snippets of left-over fabric from curtains, bedding or gift wrap.

tricks of the trade

Embellish shade papers with paint or pressed flowers and leaves (not shown) before découpaging them.

You may sandwich pressed nature materials, punched paper shapes, or stickers between two sheets of parchment paper to be découpaged.

Trim with fringe (at left) or beaded fringe, crystals, old jewelry.

The nursery is a place where "tiny" reigns. It's important to safely organize cotton swabs, safety pins, baby wipes, clean pacifiers, tweezers, thermometers, and other small items. An array of harmonizing boxes, baskets, mugs, and lidded pots make accessibility pretty and practical. Accent with colorful soaps that smell citrusy.

Select bathing items for a nursery lavatory that won't shatter when you're handling a squirming wet infant and they get knocked over. Use warp- and rust-resistant containers in a moist environment. Group the needed items so one hand can safely manage faucet, cloth, and soap, while the other holds the little one securely.

Professional designers often springboard an entire room idea from one special element. Here the curvilinear iron bed with its bunny finials sets a curvy shape to repeat in the chair back, arching mural, mirror frame, lamp base, poufy valance, and mounding curve of footstool. The bunnies abound like the ruffles that are picked up on the pillows, bed skirt, valance, and footstool base. Note how pink and lavender take turns on the iron bed and the fabrics of pillows, valance, furniture, and fabrics. Carrying out the forestry leaf pattern and stenciled words from wall murals to drawer fronts and footstool base. These delightful textural details pull the room together. The varied shapes and patterns within the palette play against neutral carpet.

Group small accessories in odd numbers. Here the lamp, the bunny, and the group of books act as three items in a group. Contrast the white bunny against the patterned lamp and books. Pink is their common color.

Whatever storybook tale is chosen for your child's room, take scale into account. Child-size furniture is basic. Select accessories that children are encouraged to hold in their small hands.

Wall art and accents must be kept to a comfortable scale, too; or when lights are dim and little eyes are sleepy, big "monsters" appear. Make audio-taped stories available to encourage "self-entertainment" apart from TV and videos, even if the electronic equipment has to be out of reach. Children learn from hearing stories before they are able to read them. Mom and dad may want to record themselves reading their children's names as characters in the stories.

A special cozy place to enjoy favorite toys and books in good light assures that your child's room will always be their favorite private place. If "time out" is necessary, make it someplace else.

Special chair

43

1. Fill and sand all surfaces to be painted. Start with coarse sandpaper and graduate to fine for last sanding. Remove dust with tack cloth.

2. Paint nightstand with selected base color. It may take several coats to cover. Allow paint to dry between coats and sand lightly with fine sandpaper before applying next coat.

3. To apply decorative color, mask off areas to be painted. Paint in unmasked areas. Remove tape.

4. For cut-out area at bottom, make paper pattern and using transfer paper, transfer design.

5. Paint as desired.

6. To make dots, use end of paintbrush.

7. Finish with at least two coats of sealer to protect piece. Let dry completely and lightly sand between each coat.

Project: Painted Nightstand

Masking tape

Nightstand

Paint – colors desired

Paintbrushes – chip brush
   – suitable to the size of the project.
   Decorative – flats, liners

Pencil

Putty knife

Sandpaper – coarse to fine

Sealer

Tack cloth

Transfer paper

Wood filler

The valance (above) has scalloped shapes that pick up the curved shapes of the other circular and curved forms in the room. The attached ruffle finishing is the same proportion in width as the bed pillows. A longer ruffle carries the treatment to the bedskirt (at right), while a tiny one accents the footstool cushion.

Pattern in a child's room can be playful. Painted furniture, as the solid-color bedframe (above) or the stencil work on the footstool base, have surprising touches. Lilac ball feet have fat spots.

tricks of the trade

Use the best brushes you can afford and keep brush strokes to a minimum. Overbrushing will leave streaks.

If a less formal look is desired, don't use tape or pattern. Freestyle is fun and you can paint over it if you don't like it.

If the piece you are working on has been painted before, remove the previous layers of paint before starting, using a paint stripper. Sand lightly, and wipe down before painting.

If you choose to paint over the previous paint, slightly roughen the original surface with fine to medium sandpaper and then use a coat of good quality primer.

Any child's environment can be made more personal when he or she has a hand in the decorating, literally as well as figuratively. More eye-catching and novel than the addition of favored toys and collectibles is the incorporation of kid-crafted arty accents. Walls, fabrics, and floorcloths can all be embellished with prints of the most personal tools of all: your child's hands, fists, and feet. For the brave and patient, even the family pets' paw prints can become whimsical design elements in a room with a personal touch.

What do you have your little hands in now?

— Susie McGruder McGlish

Rooms with a Personal Touch

Handprints may be used to create a stamp, to which paint can be applied, to "print" directly on prepainted walls or prepared fabric. Colors selected should be kept to a minimum and be related to other details used in the room. The "look" will be busy, so keep furniture and floor treatments simple and neutral.

The personal-touch theme of hand- and footprints can be especially engaging when a room is shared with two or more children. Their sense of individuality is so important to cooperative living that endorsing it in personal prints—perhaps with each little artist having their own color to print with—will support harmony in more than the room's decorative features. Separate spaces for sleeping, display, and storage are basic survival needs in sibling-shared bedrooms.

Take advantage of every storage potential when planning a room for kids whose "stuff" will seem to reproduce in number extemporaneously, as well as in size, as they grow. Pull-out bins and drawers, high and low shelving, and ingenious dual-function furniture will ease the whines about tight space. Above and below bunks and beds, window seats, and boxy furniture provide separate spaces for storage.

Hand-printed fabric can serve as bedding, valances, cushion and pillow covers, floorcloths, and lamp shade material. Towels can be hand-personalized per individual child to stave off arguments.

Hand and Foot Privacy for individual personality preferences, when accounted for in room planning, makes life an adventure rather than an endurance test for parents of children sharing a space. With a bunk above that goes its own direction, the "lower" child is also viewing "clear" to the ceiling. With two hand and foot ladder ways to access the top bunk, there's less inconvenience to the child on the bottom. In one or two foot-level drawers for each child, clothing and toys don't have to mix. Frequently used shirts, toys, and books can be shelved in the open for easy access and quick cleanups. Who isn't maintaining their space is immediately clear to parents and correctable.

1. Place cardboard under each layer of fabric to prevent paint from bleeding through.

2. Pour desired paint onto foam plate. Using foam brush, paint surface of object to be transferred onto fabric, eg.: hand, foot, or carved vegetables.

3. Place stamping object paint side down onto fabric. Press lightly. Lift straight off. Repeat process, adding paint as needed. Wash stamps during stamping process and between colors.

4. When design is completed, allow to dry and heat-set with iron or dry thoroughly in clothes dryer. Follow fabric and paint manufacturer's recommendations.

Project: Fabric Painting

Acrylic or fabric paint

Cardboard

Fabric medium

Foam brushes

Foam plates

Prewashed fabric

Rubber stamps (optional)

Sponges

Stencils

Vegetables & Fruits – potatoes, apples, mushrooms, any medium-textured fruit or vegetable (optional)

Fabric paints come in a limited number of colors, but by mixing fabric medium with acrylic paints the colors become limitless.

If using stencils, use a stencil brush and very little paint with pouncing action to prevent paint from bleeding under the stencil.

Take a favorite motif from almost anything and paint the fabric to match, such as from wallpaper, a print, or a favorite poem or storybook.

Practical, Personal Touches

Printed fabrics and wallpapers are plentiful; but in a room with personal touches, nothing's more personal than creating hand, foot, or freehand art in place of commercial wallpapers and textiles.

Fabric Choices

Certain textile materials work better for permanent fabric painting than others. Tighter weaves give a smoother surface on which to stamp or print. Natural fibers absorb paint best. Textile fabrics that perform well include: 100% cotton, burlap, cotton/polyester blends, denim, linen, silk, ultrasuede, velvet, canvas, and wool.

Tools

Children instinctively know that everything they touch is a tool for fun. Their fingers, hands, fists, feet, and elbows are effective stamping tools. Toy parts, nature materials such as leaves and stones, halved fruits and vegetables, and even the soles of an old pair of sneakers can print interesting shapes on walls and fabric. Favorite pets can even be included,

handprints

Practicing for hand- or foot-print art accents is fun for children, using thick tempra paint. When it's time for the real wall, fabric, or floor-cloth art to happen, prepare for frequent cleanups. Children will find the repetition tedious unless they can take snack and play breaks between paint sessions.

provided they are willing to have their paws dipped in paint and used to stamp. Try laying a piece of lace on fabric and lightly spraying with paint. When you lift off the lace, the imprint of the lace will be on the fabric. Any object with defining lines and shapes can be used. Commercial stamps, stencils, sponges, and transfers make great personal designs, too.

Brushes impact the look of your finished project. Fabric-painting brushes range from nylon decorative paintbrushes to stencil brushes that cover a larger area and imbed paint into the fabric. Decorative brushes give much the same look as they do on paper. Fabric pens make detail work easy and give more control for fine-line work like writing, or legs and eyes on bugs.

Techniques Specific ideas for using stamps can add interest to your wall, furniture, or textile fabric projects. Stamped materials can be used to make pillows, curtains, floorcloths, etc.

For example, glow-in-the-dark paint can make stamped stars and fireflies come to life. A special black-light bulb is required for most brands of glow-in-the-dark paints. Colors appear ordinary in natural or standard electric light illumination; but when lights are turned out, or when black-light bulbs are lit, the glowing effect happens.

Animals painted on velvet appear to have a fur-like texture. Every little princess wants jewels and glamour in her room. Decorate her favorite pillow with shimmering pearlescent, thick fabric paint that stands up in a bead effect, or use those that shine with glitter. Such dimensional fabric paint is applied through a needle-nosed applicator bottle.

Velveteen fabric paint is applied and then heated with an iron to produce a velvet finish. Children's personal art can be heat-transferred to fabric. Other products allow you to emboss glass or metal with kid's art.

Children love to see their art displayed. The esteem-building value parents make possible when giving space to their children's personal art cannot be underestimated, and it's a unique decorating resource for rooms.

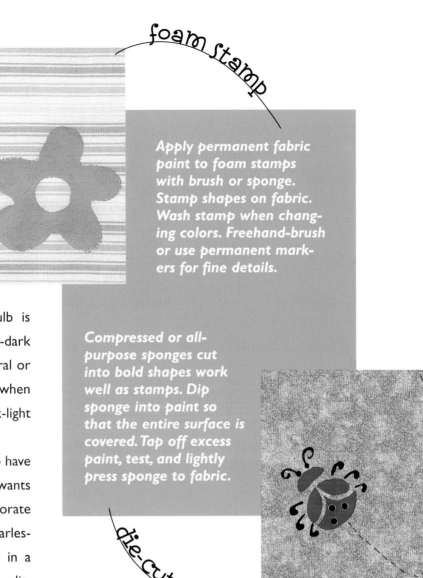

foam stamp

Apply permanent fabric paint to foam stamps with brush or sponge. Stamp shapes on fabric. Wash stamp when changing colors. Freehand-brush or use permanent markers for fine details.

Compressed or all-purpose sponges cut into bold shapes work well as stamps. Dip sponge into paint so that the entire surface is covered. Tap off excess paint, test, and lightly press sponge to fabric.

die-cut sponge

Choose fabric with texture or color variety rather than solid. Stamp shapes or draw lines randomly, or in a pattern using a rubber stamp or sponge. Detail with liner brushes or pens.

Circus, Circus, Circus It's a rare child who isn't delighted by a circus. Performing tricks in the ring (on the floor) or on the high wires (top bunk) brings out the adventurous spirit as much as showing bravery with imagined exotic animals. Circus posters, clown, and animal accents achieve this decorative look. This theme is a natural for shared spaces. Bright red and blue with touches of gold are nostalgic circus-wagon colors. The tent reference of the big top is picked up on the valance and both it and the bedding are studded with stars and circus animal shapes. The surprise feature here is that wall covering, valance, and bedding fabrics match perfectly. Who's ever seen blue wood? The circus is truly a magical place for kids.

If rustic can be as whimsical as a circus, then wall "planking" in a non-wood color, that is echoed on matching fabric bedspreads, skirts, and pillows certainly "works" for fun. Select wallpapers with matching fabric or make your own with faux treatments for walls and bedding. Colorful "paneling" can perform anywhere.

wall treatment

circus tent

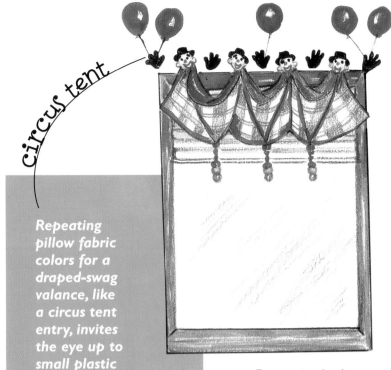

Repeating pillow fabric colors for a draped-swag valance, like a circus tent entry, invites the eye up to small plastic balloons.

Drama in the big top is played up with spotlights. The track lighting (at far left) has swivel features on each lamp to make illuminating the play table, pleasure reading in the top bunk, or playing on the circus-animal carpet a featured activity when the switch goes on. The metal ladder leading to and from the top bunk reflects the climbing equipment of high-wire acrobats.

Traveling circus performers take the show on the road. Easy-to-move furniture, in keeping with the theme, makes clearing space to practice tricks a zip for small clowns and animal trainers.

bigtop

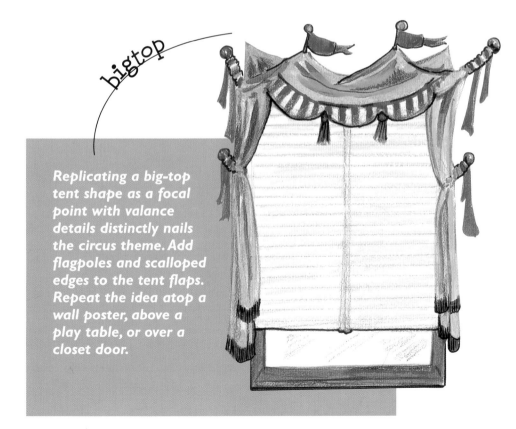

Replicating a big-top tent shape as a focal point with valance details distinctly nails the circus theme. Add flagpoles and scalloped edges to the tent flaps. Repeat the idea atop a wall poster, above a play table, or over a closet door.

Desk Idea Line a wall with lightweight sheet metal, before wallpaper goes on, for a magnetic display board that fits seamlessly into the décor. Magnetic paints are another option.

Whenever space can be created for a desk, as between these closets, an inexpensive solution is to build a shelf and add a chair, instead of buying furniture. Take the folding doors off of a long closet and rework the space like this or put a desk inside.

Boxes for storage come in every imaginable shape and size. Stick with your theme in selecting vintage suitcases, cigar boxes, or wood, metallic, and plastic boxes you can cover with découpage treatments. Monogram with names or initials.

storage boxes

An old screen door, backed with fabric-covered foam core, serves as a tidy organizer with a fresh twist. Use on a wall or as a divider. Push pins hold treasures to the screen.

Kids Display Every day is a week long for kids. Their hurts and triumphs are very big to them. Build self-esteem for your children by helping them honor themselves for their ordinary and extraordinary accomplishments. Make a place to commemorate the day they tied their shoes, took out the trash, learned their times tables, or received an honor at school, scouts, or church.

An award board "window" display focuses on bragging rights for a math, spelling, or sports star. Several kids? Create several unique-to-the-kid award boards.

56

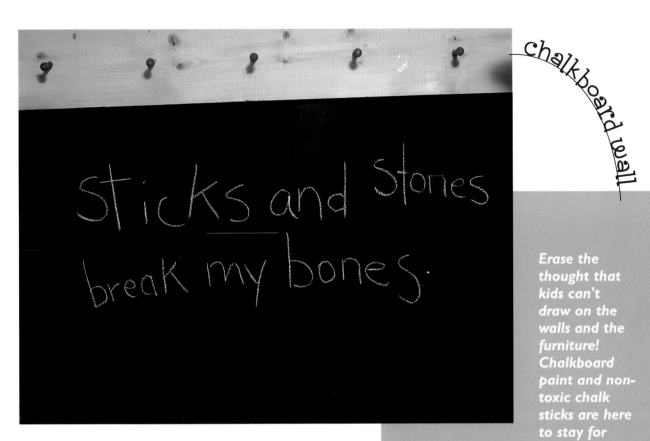

Erase the thought that kids can't draw on the walls and the furniture! Chalkboard paint and non-toxic chalk sticks are here to stay for inexpensive to "install," easy-to-clean-up fun. Dedicate wall space at least as wide as your child with arms outstretched to a chalkboard. Kids love to draw BIG or to share the experience with friends or siblings.

Painting on the Walls We can encourage our children to participate in making their environments unique to their personalities and interests. They need places to express their creativity in imaginative workshop areas you make possible. Include their participation in the ideas, preparation, wall painting, and decorating. If they help make their space special, they'll have more invested in the ownership feelings that make straightening and cleaning up less of a chore. Let them use their specially prepared walls to express their feelings and ideas.

If chalk dust doesn't appeal in your household, another inexpensive wall-drawing option is to install white, gloss-finish bath wallboard. It's lightweight and comes in 4' X 8' sheets that can be precut for you at the local lumberyard. Install with molly bolts to the wall, or screws into studs. Cover raw edges with prepainted white molding strips. Use a staple gun or epoxy for quick installation. Erase the dry-marker artwork with a dry cloth and an occasional spray of glass cleaner wiped off with a paper towel. The only drawback is that dry-markers are smelly. It is wise to crack a window in the winter and open them fully in warm weather to freshen the air quickly.

Imaginative kids' rooms sometimes have a little extra zip—some theme or design approach that sparkles in a fanciful way. The fulfillment of the design concept in such rooms often requires unique architectural or structural elements as well as out-of-the-ordinary ceiling or floor treatments. These rooms may or may not transform well from age to age for a growing child. However, the extraordinary effort and impact makes them unusually desirable.

All kids' rooms should exhibit attention to detail at every level of the room from ceiling to floor. When ingenious design, planning, and decorative execution come together, the overall effect brings a gasp of delight.

Cutting out a fresh niche in architectural design elements that merge the practical with the beautiful sometimes entails actually cutting holes or shapes in surfaces. When climbing is required, or creating doors, why not make a few solutions a bit fanciful? Shapes that are consistently squared or curved can be carried throughout a room or suite design.

The difference between ordinary and extraordinary is that little extra.

— unknown

Fanciful Rooms

Bold and perhaps unusual color helps create an extraordinary room design. There is nothing hesitant in these ideas. Dramatic geometric shapes and forms invite not only brilliant primary colors such as yellow, red, and blue, but lime green, hot orange, and purple. Reserve some large areas to be kept a neutral white or cream. Too many bright colors will overwhelm the harmony of the design. Keep the theme focus simple.

Out of This World

Shapes cut out of built-in furniture complement similar painted shapes on wall areas. The trompe l'oeil "window" to the sky (far right) imaginatively encourages the kids who share this room to feel as if they could float into space.

Seeing out a porthole in a sky-high bunk is fun. A component design approach used every inch of available space. Both bunks stair-step near the ceiling. Play areas, storage, TV, and the aquarium fit underneath. Pull-out shelves are on lock-in-place safety rollers, with fold-up doors such as the one for the aquarium (below and at right). Note its curved viewing porthole when closed. Finger-pull indentions act as handles on desk and storage pullouts.

Step down to a TV window seat (above) that doubles as guest sleeper. A hole in the wall (at left) makes the aquarium recess into the shelving unit. Portholes bring in more light.

built-in desk

Fold-up, fold-down, or slide-out parts, such as this desk, maximize space efficiency. Its dry-marker surface is a wipe-off drawing "pad." Supplies are kept on shelves and in bins below for papers, jigsaw puzzles, and play dough. Shove in bins and drawers or slide shelves in, out of the way, when playtime is over.

Little Kid to Teen Exaggerated scale in built-in furniture and decorative painting makes this room grow with the boys who live here. Remove the little kid accents. Exchange for bean-bag chairs, sofa hide-a-bed, coffee table, and big-boy hi-fi equipment. Change the pencil stool into a footstool by adding foam and fabric to the seat.

stool

Build a pencil stool. Score thin metal strips, then glue to legs. Paint as if sharpened.

Playland An imaginative play area has square porthole windows to open space. Squares repeat in table, shelf storage unit, and a cushioned hideaway box. Magritte-style art accents each "window" and will work as this child grows up. No real window? Make one big enough to sleep in! Light it from inside near the ceiling, and paint with a popcorn-cloud sky.

underwater window

Switch to a yellow submarine setting for teens. Paint an undersea window seat, add big-kid room furniture.

1. Paint box with black enamel. Let dry.

2. Paint over black enamel with red acrylic. Let black show through red. Let dry.

3. Place masking tape band around entire box, approximately 2" down from top edge.

4. Using stencil as guide along top and bottom edges, brush box with blue paint.

5. Outline stencil design with black felt-tip marker.

6. Paint bottom and lid molding with green. Let dry.

7. Paint wooden star with yellow.

8. Using pencil and wooden star for pattern, trace star onto sides and top of box. Paint stars with yellow. Let dry.

9. Lightly sand painted stars until red comes through.

10. Glue wooden star onto center of lid.

Project: Toy Box

Acrylic paints —
   blue, green,
   red, yellow

Black enamel paint

Black fine-point, felt-tip
   marker

Masking tape

Paintbrushes

Pencil

Ruler

Sand paper — coarse

Stencil

Wood glue

Wooden box with molding and lid

Wooden star

City Living Urban life-styles include intersections and airports. A landing and take-off airstrip motif in the carpet sets the theme, echoed by the airplane headboard. Mirror panels framed into the dormer-roof walls add space and light and reflect the landing strip. The pilot's bunk comes from an aircraft-carri-er idea onboard ship. Bright yellow, red, and blue keep the room young and lively. Take down the youthful toys and accents, keep the pilot's bunk and desk shelves, and a teen room flies in.

Structurally, the curved hangar-shaped bookshelf unit with its built-in desk adds authenticity to the space, which can grow beautifully to the teen years for a kid working on a pilot's license between homework assignments.

Country Living

For some imaginative families, a decorating idea has to be as big as a village. The structural elements merge with the Grandma Moses appearance of the painted walls. Buildings in the far distance are painted flat, while the larger scaled buildings appear up close with their three-dimensional moldings, shutters, picket fences, and window boxes. The firehouse takes on special importance with the wooden dalmatian rocking dog.

The firehouse sets the bright red-and-blue theme of

the room accents and furniture. Its yellow trim is picked up in trim on other village buildings and brought into the "village green" by way of the dustboard molding and the tabletop.

Numerous details such as flower trim on the picket fence, the curtains both painted and real at the windows, the chair seat designs, and red apple details say that school in the village is being held on the green today.

Transfer enlarged clip art turn-of-last-century firehouse motif to a board. Cut out and paint or use stencils or wallpaper.

firehouse

A countrified play-house little ones can go inside is believable fun at any season. Decorate from rafters to porch floor with twinkle lights and flameproof greens. Kids love doors that open, doorbells that ring, and lights that go on.

playhouse

A Very Country Christmas

If the children's bedroom has a second closet, remove the doors and create a double barn door that opens to toy shelves or bunks. Most of the playing and sleeping happens in the front yard of this playhouse. Kids will love going into their house to bring out dolls, tea sets, and small folding chairs

for the front porch (below). Even in a basement play area, this theme can be carried out with door moldings, window frames, and fence rails.

Scenic outdoor murals are only interrupted (lower far) by the room's actual window in the sky."

Grow the room to teen years with cabin getaway fishing or hunting accents.

Little girls and their bigger sisters enjoy pretty places, pretty things, and dressing up in party clothes. Even if they're only going to a tea party in their room, it's bound to be an occasion for playful elegance. It isn't necessary for a bedroom to be classically serious in order for beauty to happen. A little bit of drama, a touch of romance, and details of the feminine sort can dress up a bedroom with spirited atmosphere.

Dress up for my tea party.
— Susie McGruder McGlish

Playfully Elegant Rooms

The pretend-castle room of the little princess of your household is more comfortable than the chilly, drafty ones of fairy tales. Recall the romance of that era with lighthearted references such as "hewn stone" wall treatments, tapestry-style rugs, canopied and four-poster beds, layers of ruffled bedding, and lighting as subtle as if it came from a flickering fireplace or an antique oil lantern.

Rich jewel colors are elegant in themselves. Gold, amethyst, rose, garnet, topaz, and opalescents in their softest tints are perfect for young girls. (Save sapphire, ruby, emerald, and jet for playfully elegant teenage girls.) Use close harmony of a few related colors to restrain the busy details of rooms on the fluffy side.

Flowers are another elegant element in important rooms of the past. Floral art prints, "blossoming" wallpaper, area rugs, fabrics, and storage boxes give a visual fragrance to girls' rooms that is hard to overdo. Laces, organdy, sheers, silks, velvets, and ruffled accents of them all can be mixed and matched by keeping colors and their values analogous to one another. For playfully extravagant details, add fringed and beaded tassels, wispy swags, gold-leafed accents, and porcelain dolls.

Ball Gown Room

Tea parties were only the beginning of the social whirl for playful girls of the past. With needlework, books, music, and conversation to occupy their time, little girls looked forward to the day when they'd join their older sisters at an elegant ball. Planning and stitching gowns, then creating handmade decorative touches from the beautiful scraps, was an important aspect of growing up to be a lady.

Young girl's bedrooms can have playful reflections of bygone Cinderella days when the details that went into elegant ball gowns are imaginatively incorporated: "skirt-" and "flounce"-sashed windows, tables, beds, and footstools.

ruffled curtains

The double rows of curtain ruffles recall fabulous ball gowns. The long flow of draperies and the scallops on shade and dressing table skirt complete the "dress up" look.

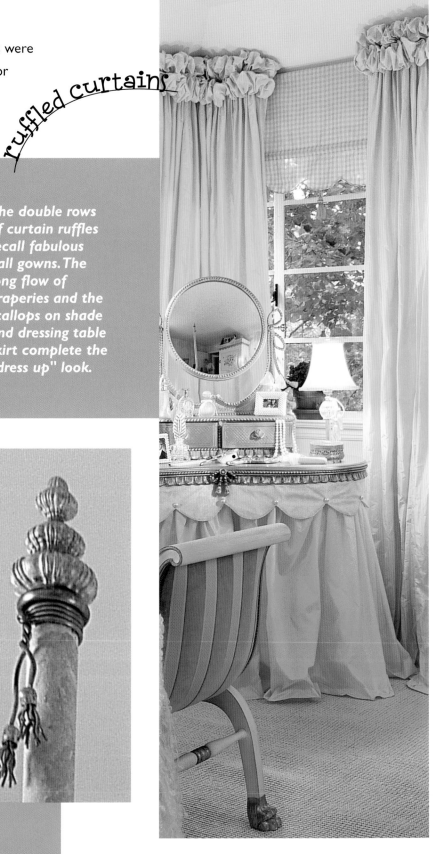

finial tassels

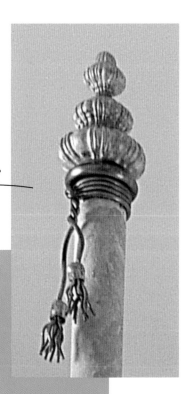

Bedpost and curtain rod finials are elegant touches. Tie fanciful tassels to their details. Repeat one on a drawer pull.

As young girls expand their social lives into the classroom and the neighborhood, keepsake photographs of friends, family, and pets gain importance. Frames of various sizes and shapes can be padded and decorated with ribbons, beads, buttons, and silk flowers in related colors. Group them as a focal point.

shelf details

floral accents

Match a fabulous floral area rug or carpet with petal details in wallpaper or bedding prints, or découpage hat and band boxes to pick up the theme.

When the need for display space or a lamp arises, maximize floor space and minimize furniture expense with a wall-mounted shelf. Face with wooden scallops. Lace, ruffles, and beaded fringe are elegant, too.

Elegant Display A glass-topped dressing table or tray to hold perfumes, makeup, lotions, and hair-care items is charming as well as practical. Open shelves can be "dressed" to hold vignette arrangements of books, framed photographs and mirrors, pretty trays, boxes of secrets, figurines, dolls, and tea sets. A padded and hinged folding screen, crisscrossed with ribbon, can display mementos, letters from friends, and souvenirs. Make the back side match, and divide a room for privacy that two girls must share. The padding helps for phone privacy and secures upholstery tacks that hold the ribbon strips.

1. Determine diamond size by measuring area to be painted and dividing it into equal portions. Use ruler and marker to make several diamonds (squares) on contact paper.

2. Using craft knife, ruler, and cutting mat, cut squares from contact paper.

3. Starting in one upper corner of room, adhere diamonds so corners meet ceiling and wall lines. Adhere diamonds across and down wall, matching at points.

4. Apply glaze where there is no contact paper square.

Note: Glaze applied over background color can be tinted with either background color or complementary color.

5. While glaze is still wet, remove contact paper. Contact paper can be reused; simply continue across and down wall, around room.

Note: Background paint should cure for at least a week so removal of contact paper does not pull up paint.

Project: Painting Diamond Wall Pattern

Applicators for glaze: sponges, rollers, rags – whatever you choose.

Black fine-point permanent marker

Clear contact paper: one roll

Craft knife

Cutting mat

Glaze

Room painted in background color

Ruler

Tape measure

A diamond wall pattern inexpensively adds a high-cost look. It is effective behind a headboard, above a vanity, or around a window seat. If you have patience, an entire wall or room is quite dramatic.

cover

Using a quilter's eye, use a 9- to 12-patch pattern to create a comforter or a cover for a goose-down insert. Can't find enough hankies? Find or stencil floral patterns and heat-transfer them to fabric "hanky" squares.

Decorating with Hankies

In times past, no little girl left home without frilly socks, an adorable hat, patent-leather shoes, and a pretty purse. Inside the purse was a special hanky, often monogrammed with her initials by a beloved grown-up. Tatted lace, embroidery, cutwork, and cross-stitch details or splashes of flowers are found on vintage and updated versions of hankies.

Collect hanky items and use them as accents in a girl's bedroom or the guest room for her young friends. Hanky edges are already finished, so framing them as art, combining them for valances, tiebacks for curtains, dresser scarves, pillow shams, and lamp-shade fabric for découpage are not time-intensive decorating solutions. Select handkerchiefs in related colors and intensities that reflect other colors in the room, or use the hankies to set the theme. Paint window frames, a footstool, or a side table to repeat a key color to harmonize the look and pull the room elements together.

hanky "curtains"

In an afternoon, and with a little girl's help, pretty new or vintage hankies can be clothespinned to ribbon or cord, or stitched and secured with button tabs or rings to a tension rod.

1. Pin hankies together so they overlap slightly. Arrange in four rows of four hankies each.

2. Sew hankies together, removing pins as you go. You have just created a pretty blanket top.

3. Cut flannel to exact dimensions of blanket top.

4. With right sides together, pin blanket top to flannel.

5. Sew seams together, removing pins as you go. Leave 4"–5" opening. Iron seams of blanket so that they lie flat. Turn blanket rightside out. Slip-stitch opening shut.

Project: Hanky Blanket

Coordinating flannel – two yards

Coordinating thread

Hankies – sixteen

Iron/ironing board

Scissors

Sewing machine

Sewing needle

Straight pins

Frame a particularly beautiful vintage hanky on a contrasting colored matte for unusual wall art.

Create a soft window valance by using thumbtacks to loosely drape hankies across the top of a window.

A baby's crib pillow is easily made by sewing two hankies together, back to back and inserting a pillow form.

Tea Party Time In the room of a little girl, or two, who still love to play dolls, there simply must be everything needed for a tea party. A mini tea vignette for toys creates a tea party setting. Include doll and toy-size furniture big enough for a little girl to join her toy guests. Soft pastel furniture and beautiful bedding pretty enough to be made into doll clothes are theme stealers here. Too young for make-up, the dressing table is charming enough for a young girl to grow into, while it reflects her twirling dress-up skirt.

Stencil and Plaid Surprise

Floral print and plaid patterns combine for whimsy at a delightful level. Stencil designs on walls, head- and footboards, mirror frame, drawer fronts, and chair back complement the bed skirt. Plaid fabric découpaged to the wall and top drawer fronts repeats on the padded footstool. Lilac paint is sassy on wood accents.

footstool

Lathe-turned legs invite painted stripes and tassel accents. Stuff or overstuff the top.

The Elegance of Flowers Unique floral stencils at the ceiling corners (at left) are a delightfully unexpected theme detail. Note how the flowers are in bouquets as well as trailing arrangements that frame a charming curve on the mirror and repeat that arch above and over the bed to finish the plaid wall focal points of both areas. Bands of flowers on drawers and chair back take yet another stencil shape. Variety within this stencil design unity makes this room unique.

flower accents

The floral-print bed skirt fabric echos the palette of the stenciled flowers and the squares within the plaid. Color is the unifying element between dissimilar patterns and paint.

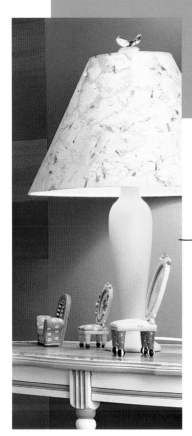

In the full light of the lamp, miniature chairs pick up colors in the room into one little focal point.

doll furniture

flower bench

A child-size bench with a picket-fence back and mini pillows invites a play doll or a real one to sit and put on shoes. Finish the doll's "garden" with flower cutouts on the bench front. Grow a few wooden ones on the wall.

If dolls or flowers are mixed into your little girl's theme room, accessory possibilities are unlimited. Scale of doll accent items kept comparatively small is best.

Area rugs with floral designs set a theme to be picked up in fanciful wood cutouts. Use them as doorknobs, drawer pulls, backing for clothing hooks—even for hanging doll clothes by the doll play area.

Rose Bower Princess An elegant corniced ceiling fixture secures a scalloped canopy and its swags, festooned with bows at the four bedposts. It calls for a chandelier to drape with beaded swags. The young girl dreams here in a bower of pink and celadon rose-bedecked wallpaper. Pink is picked up in the ceiling, a contrasting foil for the cornice. Stained-glass suspended in front of a mirrored window makes a bleak view disappear, while sweet room drama repeats in roses and swags.

Double framing art with gold is the epitome of bygone beauty. Arrange symmetrically in pairs, with a whimsical surprise, such as a hat, framed gloves, or a high-button shoe.

frames

bead accents

Bead accents emit sparkles of grandeur in this hanging lamp shade. Ensure the look at a secret price. Visit craft and thrift shops for vintage lamps, holiday bead strands, pendants, and beaded fringe. String, wire, or glue them yourself. Add ribbon bows. Embellish a hanging fixture.

While you and your child may have very different ideas of what makes beautiful art, even your child's more unusual art selections can be framed artistically and hung in your child's room. Also, you can use this as an opportunity to introduce them to the Masters through prints and postcards. A trip to your local museum will open their eyes to new worlds of artistic choices.

Elegant Furniture Select furniture with long-term use in mind. Perhaps, your girl will fall in love with an especially beautiful and functional chest, curio cabinet, desk or armoire that she's enjoyed as a child. She may beg to take it along when she grows up and leaves home. Restore and embellish a found piece, if affording "new" elegance is financially prohibitive. The stripping, sanding, painting, glazing, stenciling, and decorating will be well worth it.

Storage

Antiquing a piece of vintage furniture combines beauty and helps with storage. Add stenciled flower designs on the sides, on the scalloped base, and across the top cornice. Put a mirror on the door and hang a tassel. Dress the top. Voila, an elegant focal point!

Elegant details support the rose-bower theme. The white-painted headboard and bed-posts have découpaged or painted nosegays of rosebuds. The lamp shade gets a top band of flowers and a lacy edge of beads. A small metal bistro table comes in from the garden to support the bower idea, with birds on a sculpted vine. It is complemented by an embossed metal shabby-chic style picture frame and a rescued cup and saucer "vase," for a single warm-tone blossom. Satin and lace pillows and gingham bolster establish comfy elegance.

over the top

An ornate frame found in a flea market and painted white holds a mirror. Hang it above a contrasting dark-finished desk. Tie together with pairs of wall pockets, white lamps, a surprising white metal chair with a ruffled cushion, and a white pot of white flowers—doubled in the mirror. White embraces dark.

lace

Lace trims in a variety of widths and colors, thrift-shop-rescued lace, and lacy hankies make delicate decorative tiebacks for a feminine room.

Trims that have flowers make a spring daisy or Old World rose romantic statement. Silk flowers also can be tucked into lace for precise color matches to wallpaper or fabric.

flowers

Tiebacks Whether curtains are tied back all of the time as decorative touches or some of the time for practical use, they are among the quick and charming room accents that can change with the age, gender, and taste of your child. They can be expensive investments, but certainly don't have to be, as those pictured and suggested here attest.

Wall hooks and plastic or metal rings stitched to the ends of the tiebacks are a convenience you'll want if the curtains are released some of the time for privacy and closing out the daylight. If however, the curtains are tied back high, low, or in the center all of the time, then a wall hook may be all you need. The tiebacks can be loops that are stitched closed and just catch at the back over the hooks.

Whatever tieback solution you choose, this perfect little place to reinforce your theme with an attention to detail won't go unnoticed. Tiebacks can be made of any materials from rugged to elegant to fit the age, gender, and taste of your child. They can be easily changed.

Surprising tieback touches can be of the jewelry type. For a girl or a boy, a tieback can be a favored beaded bracelet or a cowboy belt, with an interesting buckle, looped a few times.

A fabric tieback made from curtain material gets an extra punch with the addition of tiny plastic charms and dime-store rubber balloons.

1. Prewash and dry fabric item. Pretreat with alum mordant color-retention agent to set color permanently.

2. Heat large pot of water to boiling. Add 10 tea bags. Steep for 5–10 minutes.

3. Submerge fabric item in tea bath. Let sit for 20 minutes.

4. Remove fabric item. Rinse in cool water. Towel off excess.

5. Dry item in dryer to permanently set color. Iron.

Note: Test on fabric scrap for desired vintage color.

Project: Tea Staining

Alum mordant

Tea bags – ten
different teas produce
different hues:
Green tea – yellow
Black tea – light tan
Berry tea – pale pink
Coffee – warm brown

Select item in natural fiber
material

Natural fibers or cotton/polyester blends are best for absorbing tea or coffee.

Adding 10 additional tea bags to a pot of water produces a deeper color, but adding more than 20 does not make a significant difference in color depth.

For an alternative, follow the directions above but substitute strong coffee.

Achieve mottled effects by blotting tea or coffee onto portions of fabric, instead of submerging entire item.

Rustic folk-art rooms transition beautifully from nursery to almost-grown-up when you make wall, ceiling, and floor treatments work with a few well-planned changes. Sophistication grounded in country comfort is lively with rustic wood and folk-art accents. Bent willow and natural wood furniture is compatible with carved and painted-wood farm or wilderness imagery. Patriotic and country practical accents from settler days are updated with today's craft techniques and materials.

Country recalls farming. Even the most advanced farms are dependent upon sunshine and water to sustain plants and animals. Stars, suns, moons, garden shapes, and domesticated animals support this look. It includes light or fitting imagery for the cycles of the seasons, appropriate to the age of your child.

Allegiance to God, country, family, and the land shaped a hard but simple life in Colonial times. It is still so in many farming communities. Rustic folk-art theme rooms pay homage to those simple and important values. Accents are simple and bold. But just as farm folk are risk takers, so is the design approach to this theme. Nostalgia and whimsy soften the hard edge of work with a sense of down-home humor and tongue-in-cheek exaggeration.

Life is filled with as many possibilities as there are stars in the sky.

— unknown

Rustic Folk Art Through the Years

Fabrics here are the natural ones that once came from home-spun fibers. Gingham, wool, cotton, denim, linen, chintz, and burlap show up in rustic rooms. Green—the color of growing things—is popular in shades from muted to brilliant. High contrast is a primary look, even where the colors range from grayed to putty tones. Wood in furniture, floors, beamed ceilings, wainscoting, paneling, and accent items appears in stained as well as painted versions and is often stenciled.

Room as a Nursery Planning long-term for this folk-art theme room included a pair of removable bentwood headboards for the twin beds, appropriate for siblings sharing a room or one child and a guest. A rustic bassinet is backed by one of the headboards for the infant's nursery. Without altering the painted walls and their imagery, or the wood-framed mirror, a shelf can be hung above the changing table to keep necessaries within reach. Safety rails on both furniture pieces match the appearance of the rustic headboard and mirror. Taking a cue from the stars and heart images on the wall, a floorcloth of painted canvas pulls the whimsical charm of the theme to ground level. A skirt disguises changing-table storage shelves.

For a new-born angel who stars in this nursery, painted wooden cut-outs and découpaged stars and heart details are lively.

infant

Enhance a store-bought diaper pail or covered bin with repeated, découpaged theme images.

Focus the busy energy of 2–7-year-olds in the design elements and keep the clutter of "stuff" to a minimum. Headboards star for two with outdoor charm.

Room for Two 2-7-year-olds

Energy is high and attention spans are short. Folk-art shapes stimulate children who recognize and learn the animal names quickly, and broaden their world with meanings. Fabrics are comfortable and washable. Colors are cheerful. Nothing has changed since nursery days except the cribs and changing table went out and the beds and side tables came in. Stories, from great grandpa on the farm to *Chicken Little* and *The Three Pigs*, bring smiles here.

Timeless Wood Accents

Wood has become so threatened as a precious resource that scraps we might once have thrown on the woodpile are eagerly sought by furniture makers and artisans.

Look for unique lathe-turned accent items to celebrate the beauty of all species of wood. Rustic furnishings and sculpture may even have bark, knotholes, and knobby branches incorporated for texture. Keep focal arrangements with such pieces simple so that fine subtleties are not lost.

rustic furniture

Rustic furniture is quickly snapped up in shops. You may want to make your own or start with unfinished pieces. With a parson's table idea, this rustic version in peeled-branch components looks at home up town or in the country. Dress it simply for baby or big boys and girls. It will grow with the room until empty nest time says kids are college age.

directions

1. Stain mirror frame to desired shade.

2. Using saw, cut twigs to fit around mirror and outside edge of frame. Carefully split twigs lengthwise to give one flat side if desired.

3. Cut four twigs to fit between side pieces of frame.

4. Cut four twigs to fit between mitered corners of frame.

5. Glue twigs in place onto mirror. Allow glue to dry.

Project:
Wood Mirror

materials

Handsaw

Mirror with wide wooden frame

Wood glue

Wood stain – desired shade

Wood twigs – ¾" to 1" dia.

The custom rustic appearance of this mirror is timeless. It transitions well between ages of children and room styles from folk art to rustic, Western, and wilderness. The commanding size of such a mirror is an anchoring focal point that sets and reflects the charm of a rustic theme.

Room for an 8-14-year-old The pre-teen to early teen years bring explosions of individual interests and social activities, that include close friends. Travel interests and fun inspired a transition from folk art to whimsical Southwest with gecko delights.

The daisies on the wall become fanciful cactus blossoms with stencils or freehand cactus plants. Stars in the night sky remain, as do

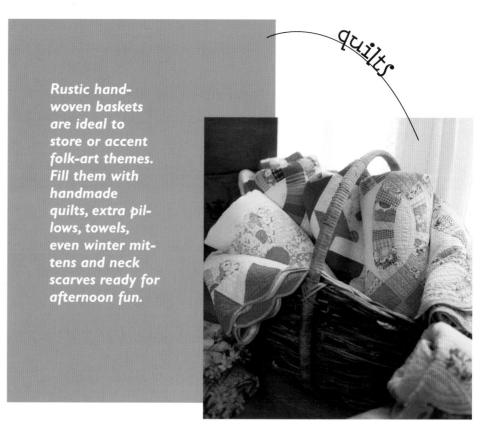

quilts

Rustic handwoven baskets are ideal to store or accent folk-art themes. Fill them with handmade quilts, extra pillows, towels, even winter mittens and neck scarves ready for afternoon fun.

the sheep, but others change from the domestic to the wild variety. Painted wooden stars on the headboards get a switch to geckos (at far right). Colorful creatures are repeated in oversized stuffed pillows that serve as floor cushions for entertaining friends. The wooden chair gets lightening arrow details (at far right), repeated from the drawer fronts of side tables. Track lighting is directional for spotlighting deskwork, reading in bed, or playing board games on the floor. Separate dimmer switches on the wall (not shown) allow child and overnight guest to control light intensity in their space. So far, few changes in walls and only stars changed to geckos in furniture.

The stars-and-stripes chair works as an old-time theme for folk art, Western, or Americana. Paint an old or unfinished chair, add painted wooden stars and heart shapes. Repeat flag elements in pillows or floorcloth. If using in room at right, keep the flag (page 89) on the sheep's hip.

Repaint chicken to roadrunner, cat to puma, pig to rabbit, stars to geckos, etc. Bring back the nursery floorcloth. Add mirrored shelves for CDs and books.

8-14 years old

Room for 15-year-olds to College Age

The element of surprise is especially important to teens and young adults. Their minds and experience are expanding. They think about concepts bigger than themselves, such as the sky, space and undersea exploration, ancient cultures, and philosophy. They begin to select friends who "get it," not just continue to hang out with the kids they've grown up with. It might be easier for parents to keep tabs on their teens by increasing the interest in their home space. Help them create a room for computer use, their kind of music, entertaining friends, as well as kicking back in privacy, style, and comfort.

As young people observe their world, their passions often run to the preservation of the environment and appreciation for natural resources. Rustic, "straight from nature" aged wood and carved wood accents appeal to them in new ways. Their spaces reflect ideas.

The dark wall top was repainted with metallic paint (at far right), then given a midnight blue top coat. Removable magnetized stars sparkle under black-lighting provided by changeable track bulbs. Reflective tape as constellation-marker strips connects the stars. Bear, wolf, and lightening arrows are power symbols in music and art.

Girls or guys want shelves to keep their stuff separate from their siblings'. Display their collections and hobbies as part of a unifying theme. Bears and wolves pop up here in useful accents.

bookends

wooden vase

Rustic containers are unique accents that merge nature with expressive sophistication.

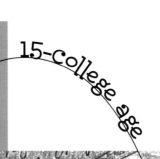

A teen intrigued with star constellations changed a Southwest idea to a bear and wolf theme. Black-lighting "lights up" stars to share with an overnight guest.

If your kids' favorite activities involve getting physical, they need plenty of room to move and to store their variety of sports equipment. Picking a theme to express their athleticism is a matter of narrowing their interests to a couple of activities. If that is tough for your children, help them focus on one indoor and one outdoor sport. If they are earning trophies and ribbons in several sports, the room may take on an eclectic sweep of several of their skills.

We can't control the winds, but we can adjust our sails.

— unknown

Sporty Rooms

Select all surfaces in washable materials. Minimalist design approaches are favored for sporty rooms. Built-in furniture or movable sturdy items only. Leave out the draperies, tiebacks, bed skirts, and other high-maintenance details. Bed sacks, slip-covered mattresses, roll-up rugs or blankets with nonskid backing strips are various ways to make a room easy care and ready in an instant for a wrestling match. In-wall vacuum systems are flip-a-switch easy for after-game popcorn cleanup.

Just because it's going to be sporty doesn't mean it has to look like a locker room, though that's a fine idea. Narrow the theme focus to one or two sports. The supportive details will come together with the equipment it takes to participate. Giant posters of their sports heroes in game uniform are popular with kids and can endorse a theme with details for floors, storage, door, and closet ideas. Plan for a comfortable place for teammates to kick back between practices.

Sporty kids are the least likely to want to spend a lot of time in their rooms, unless they can be watching sports on TV or playing competitive video games. Select materials and treatments for floors, walls, storage, and comfort that are easy to maintain. These active kids are eager to get out the door with a skateboard, a bike, or every piece of equipment it takes to play their favorite game.

Sport Accents The beautiful hardwood floor and bunk support (below) would recall a well-swabbed deck, even without a sailboat and ship's structural details. If your athletic kid's space has a stunning architectural element, establish an important component of your design thrust with it, and sublimate the other elements, such as "steel" white walls (as opposed to colorful ones)

growth chart

Buy or enlarge a poster (on paper or fabric) to life-size of the star athlete. Make a growth chart of your kid's evolving measurements with markers.

The sporty theme of this room is set with simple but effective "ship girder" or locker room details above bunk and doorway. Circle cutouts were traced from coffee tins onto particle board shapes. The door shapes were spray-painted white and combined with **PVC®** pipe decorative uprights.

Lots of Storage A wall of built-in storage for a variety of clothing and sports equipment is ideal when combined with a study desk and bookshelves. Front all components in matched scrubbable surface treatments and unfussy door and drawer pulls. Even TV and computer equipment can await use behind doors on pull-out shelves. Minimizing distractions when it's time to keep the grade-point average up to stay on the team is a way to help young athletes stay focused at a simple practical desk.

A favorite team pennant and a sailboat maintain a sporty theme. It wouldn't take a nautical enthusiast to appreciate the "keep it shipshape" ease of this clean-cut space. This place-for-everything room with built-in features is a winner for an athlete.

window seat

For kids who think all white is too stark, and everything stowed behind closed doors is boring, introduce color in fabrics, boxes, and baskets. The window seat (above left) gets another cushioned level. It allows for open storage above and pull-out storage below the window seat.

Transitioning Spaces   If the luxury of a teen suite with bath exists for your young athlete, it's an ideal situation for everyone in the family. Showers before and after sporting events and athletic practices often call for cleanup to happen at home. An athlete's shower area will get twice the ordinary use.

When decorating the bedroom and shared space between one room and an

Avoid tape on the walls. Adhere or heat-transfer favorite posters to fabric window-shade panels on two poles. On sunny days, these heroes really shine. Slide panels to each side for sunshine.

adjoining bathroom, select materials that transition well. Consider wet areas, nonslip surfaces, phone cords, hampers, towel bars, and supplies for showering and dressing in privacy.

The variables of such spaces increase the design and convenience considerations. The ease of living with sporty types who would leave wet towels behind in the family bath is well worth the planning and expense of an extra bath.

Wall colors should repeat in both areas, though floor treatments will differ. Tiles and bath fixtures in mature taste assist the room transition well into when it hosts the college athlete.

Teens' Sporty Hangout This room's outstanding architectural feature is space with light at more than one level. The floor doesn't have to be gorgeous hardwood, but it can receive a ready-for-rugged paint treatment to reflect all that light and keep the simple uncluttered statement clear. With white walls, floors, and window blinds, an absence of curtains and shelves to keep things off the floor, this room welcomes a teen and his friends.

Art can be posters or a kid's self-portrait, but keep it simple. Shelves for trophies and memorabilia are necessities. Computer equipment and video games, bikes, skateboards, and places to study can share space if furniture is kept simple.

Though there's plenty of natural light from windows, ambient, safety, and task lighting for cloudy days and evenings is an important consideration. Canisters in ceilings may be halogen or other lamp types, focusable in specific directions or fixed; but they need to be there.

Sporty teens and their friends tend to run up and down stairs, slide across floors, and collide with each other and too much stuff. An absence of rugs and unnecessary furniture just makes everyone's life safer and less stressful. Imposing your decorative tastes on an all-out athlete may place parents on a losing-battle team. Keep the maintenance simple.

Get a built-in look with stacked cubes. Arrange stair-step fashion and make space for everything from books to stereos, shoes, and trophies. Color them hot in wipe-clean paint. Cover outsides with washable vinyl wallpaper.

Storage

Sports Fan If your kid is wild about collecting souvenirs of favorite sports, you are in luck for decorating.

Collectors need display space. It might as well be up out of the way and make a practical architectural statement at the same time. Design-savvy shelves, pegboards, hooks, and knobs are useful display solutions.

Neutral wall tones, bold shapes and colors, and soft fabrics fit the spectator sportsman. He watches and replays games in comfort.

band box

Images from a fan's passion transform a box or container into an archive for a collector's player cards, pins, or photos. Découpage hand-colored cutouts or wallpaper to papier maché boxes. Glue on trims and ornaments. Project directions on page 23.

1. Cut both fabrics into squares 2" larger than pillow form.

2. Pin and sew flag to center of denim. Remove pins.

3. Using yarn and embroidery needle, sew large slip stitches around flag.

4. With right sides together, pin and sew fabric squares together, leaving 5"–6" opening in center of one side.

5. Turn pillow covering right side out.

6. Insert pillow form.

7. Hand-stitch pillow opening shut with matching thread.

8. Using yarn and embroidery needle, sew large slip stitches around edges of pillow.

Project: Flag of the Athlete

Denim fabric

Matching thread

Matching yarn

Needles – embroidery, sewing

Polar fleece fabric

Scissors

Sewing machine

Small flag

Square pillow form

Straight pins

Kids imagine themselves heroes of their fantasies: riding on horses to herd steers or capture bank robbers, rescuing puppies, going off on safari to see wild animals, or driving race cars to the finish line for trophies. Borrow decorating ideas from these rustic to refined "wild" room samplings. From ceiling to floor level, each element plays an important role in making the entire room "work."

Begin your assessment of how your child's bedroom can reflect their adventurous goals by considering their interests and all the room's architectural features. Window, door, wall, ceiling, and floor elements each have potential to be exploited in fresh ways before furniture and accents are incorporated.

Though there is often only one focal point in the transformed room, any design components included should support the atmosphere and theme appropriate to the age of the child. Every careful grouping of furniture, accessories, and art should support an inviting harmony. Especially for out-of-the-ordinary "wild" room themes, make dramatic use of an inspiring key item that sets the mood and can have its shape, color, texture, or image repeated elsewhere.

You are the hero of your own story.
— Mary McCarthy

Rooms on the Wild Side

The uneven surface of shag carpeting can frustrate little ones who build block towers or spin toy wheels across a room. Take into account the intended use and age of users of floors for spreading out games, running trucks, or learning pop dance moves. Consider sound transfer to other rooms and cleanup ease when selecting flooring. White and light colors are fine if carpets are stain-treated. Laminates and vinyls are easily cleanable. Purchase the best you can afford for long-term durability.

Teen's Room Doubling as a conversation area, the hide-a-beds welcome overnight friends. Light captured from dormer window is sent around the room by the mirrored walls, dramatically expanding the space and repeating lively pillow accents. Movable furnishings make quick space for dancing, jam sessions, and workout equipment.

Cola cases became the support for a unique triangular coffee table for a youthful attitude. Transparent surfaces emphasize open-space effects. Plexiglas® can be cut to any shape of top. For a base: outgrown toys, car parts, or glued-together bowling balls may also be used.

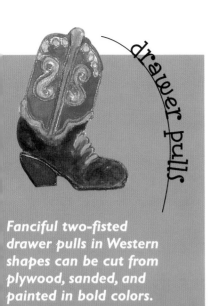

Fanciful two-fisted drawer pulls in Western shapes can be cut from plywood, sanded, and painted in bold colors.

young cowboy What kid hasn't imagined riding horses and living on a ranch in the Old West? Active young cowpokes need plenty of room to gallop around the play table and spread out some toys. Make-believe is still very real to them. Pretending and having fun are important aspects of children's developing imaginations. Western details rope-in this theme with practical panache.

Keep toys and books within easy reach on wall-bolted shelving. Bright colors invite exploration of skill-building toys. Cleaning plastic furniture is "spray and wipe" easy, as are nontoxic enamel-painted surfaces. Shelving and drawers under window seats and beds double the storage space.

Bunkhouse

A bold, simply furnished bunkhouse room is just the place for cowboy kids to hang their hero hats.

Cover ceiling tiles with fabric for display squares. Mounted diamond style, they brand the walls of young mavericks with art of their own. A steer-skull accent can be the real thing or a molded-resin replica complemented by a boot that could even hold a planter of cacti.

Paired items: wooden bedsteads with theme-coordinated comforters, task lamps, and wall display boards echo the simple ranch style of the past. The parson's-style table serves as a homework space with knee room for two buckaroos. Ladder-back chair and wainscoting link the space together as neatly as a rail fence.

A cowpoke's hat is traditionally on his head or within reach. Riders have their work hats. Rodeo stars take pride in their parade hats. Every cowboy or girl has one or a herd of them. Lasso the cowboy-hat theme with decorative art accents in wood and metal, or display the real things right out in the open.

Cowboy charm

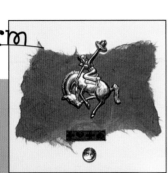

A brass charm bronco rider on a handmade paper note card is fun door panel art.

A rescued antique or "faux-painted to look aged" window frame makes a focal point hat rack. With the addition of a few pegs, your kid can hang as many hats as he or she owns.

Cow punchers with fewer hats can hang fringed jackets, ribbon shirts, wide-brimmed sombreros, chaps with concha accents, woven serapes, leather crops, and Indian blanket icons of the old and new Southwest.

For another window frame variation on this one, mount mirrors in empty pane spaces (not shown). It expands space by reflecting light and repeating Western room decorations.

Western rooms sport leather boots, saddles, and weathered wood details. Complement them with refined accents: civilized fine art and handcrafted items such as heat-transfer or needlework pillow designs and colorful rag throw rugs.

Metal sheeting cut into switch plates and decorative items can enhance a theme. Distress each plate with hammer dents and nail scratches, then antique or paint them to match your color scheme.

switch plates

Rustic distressed wood, and rough-sawn planking have a Wild West flavor. Mismatched legs on the window table declare "anything goes in the great outdoors."

Store boots, hats, and saddles outside the closet for a "rough and ready at a moment's notice" cowboy attitude.

Repeat the antique-window-frame idea as a picture frame for a series of prints to unify a Western-style room. Uniformly matted, nostalgic cowboy images depict ordinary ranch activities. Be certain to include a posse queen or rodeo princess if a cowgirl bunks here.

Checks and plaids work well in Western rooms for boys; gingham, chintz, or velvet fabric with beaded trim appeals to girls. Enhance with fringe for both genders.

Use a jigsaw to cut out a pair of wooden, bucking bronco bookends. Sand and seal or paint them for a rustic and practical accent.

bookends

There's a "kick back" attitude about casual yet sophisticated room décors for a pre- or older teen. Use rugged materials, strong simple forms and colors, and "collectible" decorative details to set a masculine atmosphere. For "outdoorsy" girls, add horse- or fishing-related ribbons, soft fabrics, beads, and denim ruffles.

A fence-slat footboard on the bed (below) adds a rounded repeat pattern to contrast with squares in the designs of the wall-hung quilt, checked carpet, and theme pillows. Stripes in curtains and bedspread echo the quilt's strong verticals and horizontals. If a life-size bear cub doesn't do it for your child, a faux-painted bear or fish floorcloth or fringed rawhide rug would be at home here. Rough rugs or wall art "tapestries" can be made from leather trimmings stitched to a fabric "hide" shape.

Chunky leather club chairs, sheepskin throws, trout designs, and waterfowl decoys bespeak a teen that enjoys hunting and fishing. Though a preserved-under-glass antique flag is the focal point of this room, an artfully weathered wilderness map or a collection of fishing rods and lures, or outdoor photographs of the "heroes" in action could serve as well.

mobile. Behind the crib, a wall-mounted cornice header has antique treatment. The baby's name is framed (far left) with birth information and hung above the window seat. Alphabet flash cards were the resource for heat-transfer animals on some pillows. Velvet, suede, toile, and linen were carried out in the inlay designs of valance, quilt, bumper, and crib-tie accents. The bear clock mimics the mobile and accents the whimsical animal theme.

animal valance

Tiny stuffed-animal toys secured to each pleat are charming accents. Crystal beads for the hem can be inexpensive craft varieties you string yourself.

"Refined Rustic" Nursery

Who says nurseries have to be pink, blue, or pastel in color palette?

With but few ruffle accents and crystal pendants on lamp shades and valances, this room is baby-charming for either gender, while not too sweet. Earth tones of fabric, bindings, and fringe complement the restored antique furnishings. Attention to detail includes wee animals that stud the pleated valance and

Wild-animal images have been used on the pillow material (at left). Embellish with fabric paints, or use cross-stitch or needlepoint animal pillows as other "wild" options.

Refined-rustic, wildlife-correct animal elements grow with the child in this rustic nursery themed into an Audubon-style room. Sophisticated styling spells B-E-N in wild-animal alphabet prints. A birth information plate is set into the classic matte. Repeated graceful capital letters on the animal pillows draw the eye back to the wall prints. Even if beyond learning the alphabet, personalized decorating tells BEN that he's important. His last name could be spelled out on the pillows, bedding, or on custom-painted drawer knobs.

A girl would be equally at home here. Beautiful earth colors, feather and fur visual textures, and animal forms harmonize with wood antiques and a lamp with animal-carving accents.

Game Room Board games are simple in design; they emphasize squares. They also proceed from player to player in step fashion. Bedrooms designed around variations on board games are uncluttered and orderly and ageless.

drawer pulls

Circular wooden checker pieces, centered with chess knights, create delightful drawer pulls or swag holders.

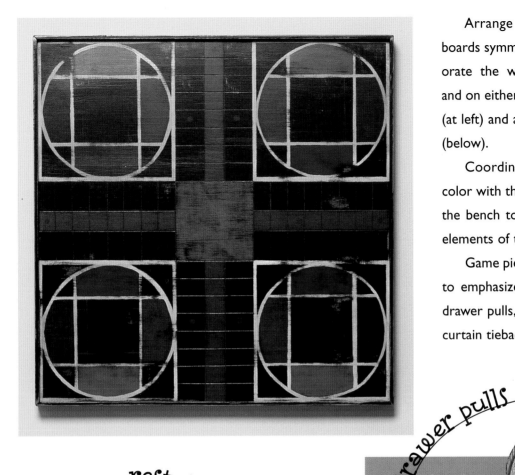

Arrange square game boards symmetrically to decorate the walls, one above and on either side of the bed (at left) and above the bench (below).

Coordinate the frame color with the wood paint of the bench to harmonize the elements of the room.

Game pieces can be used to emphasize the theme on drawer pulls, doorknobs, and curtain tiebacks.

drawer pulls

Attach a marble to a checker piece.

restyled table

What was once a coffee table has been transformed into a padded bench. Its original top was removed, then a reinforced, padded seat was added and covered in checked plaid fabric matching the bed, but in a contrasting color.

Safari Kids can imagine themselves in Africa in a safari tent. From floor to ceiling, fabric on the end window wall is continuous. Tent-like, a roll-down shade combines all windows into one. The ceiling cornice replicates a tent frame. The faux-painted "animal skin" area rug gives canvas a wild new twist. The wilderness-refuge idea comes to life with wood and wicker furniture, hanging "shelves" (lest the pretend floor critters get into kids' snacks), and animal-print fabric pillows. The hero's pith helmet hangs on a folding chair, adding to the illusion that the "camp" moves out on safari at dawn. Roll up the canopy, dismantle the tent, and move out.

1. Using foam brush, apply gesso with brush to pattern side of floorcloth.

2. Using foam brush, paint floorcloth with flesh. Let dry.

3. Using painter's tape, mask off 3" border on all four sides of floorcloth.

4. Paint border with spice tan. Leave tape in place. Let dry.

5. Pour small amount of black paint on plate. Using cosmetic sponge, tap paint onto tiger print stamp. Stamp entire border, reapplying paint after each impression. Remove tape.

6. Using masking tape, create nine diamonds in the center of floorcloth.

7. Paint diamonds with spice tan. Leave masking tape. Let dry.

8. Tap black paint onto leopard-print stamp. Stamp painted diamonds, reapplying paint after each impression. Remove tape.

9. Using liner paint thin black border around tiger print pattern. Let dry.

10. Using flat paintbrush, apply 3–4 coats matte varnish.

11. Using foam brush, paint reverse side of floorcloth with flesh. Let dry.

12. Using flat paintbrush, apply 3–4 coats matte varnish on reverse side of floorcloth.

Project: Animal-print Floorcloth

Acrylic paints – black, flesh, spice tan

Canvas floorcloth – 38" X 29"

Cosmetic sponges

Foam brushes

Foam plates

Foam stamps – leopard print, tiger print

Gesso

Masking tape

Matte varnish

Painter's tape – 1"

Paintbrushes – flat, liners

Water

zebra picture

Paint a wood square with one coat each of white, yellow, and black. Scratch design through layers with a screwdriver. Add an animal cutout or stamp.

Animals, Animals, Animals

Designed for heroes home between safaris, because they're not old enough to go without their parents, this room spells adventure. Cheetah-print fabrics, border patterns and textures on wall mirror and area rug, stuffed wild animals, and animal art are wild for the young set. A woven trunk doubles as a display table for "trophies." Masculine harmony comes from dark rich colors, ceiling cornice, and wainscoting.

You're Ready

Decorating your child's room will be successful. Now you are armed with new concept and decorating ideas, technique suggestions, and projects you can make. You've learned factors that make a kid's room comfortable and beautiful, as well as safe, functional, and economical.

Your new space-saving and storage ideas can be created with built-in furniture, drawers, bins, and shelving. Examples of rooms that are to be shared by two or more children have provided practical and creative solutions to everyday challenges.

You've explored rooms from infant to toddler, young child to preteen, and from the high-school age to the college-age young adult. With suggestions from *Great Kids' Rooms*, you've learned how to take a basic room and some carefully selected timeless furniture and, with a few decorative accent changes, transform it to work beautifully for your child at any age.

We've offered examples of many different themes appropriate to each age child, but more importantly, helped you think of how to come up with fresh ideas that may be closer to the interests of your child. Special storage and decorative projects that really function are in your bag of theme tricks as well.

Enjoy every process in the transformation of your children's rooms, now that you're equipped to be the great decorator of kids' rooms at your house.

you've learned!

We've considered the entire space with which you have to work—from ceiling to floor treatments, walls to windows, and trims, decorative accents that support the focal point of special furniture or theme art.

You're Prepared to Get Started

Acknowledgments

The publishers wish to thank the following for use of their products, homes, businesses, or photographs:

A.I. Paper Design
3117 West Twelve Mile
Berkley, MI 48072
Photo Albums p. 37(ur), Picture Frame p. 37(ur)

Antique Reflections
1208 Isabel Street
Burbank, CA 91506
Wooden Plaques p. 22(u)

Bathology
7980 Capwell Drive
Oakland, CA 94621
Soap p. 41(b)

Bella Notte
20 Galli Drive, #E
Novato, CA 94949
Pillow p. 25(r), Pillow p. 31(r)

Blue Moon / Send Me A Dream
9835 Max Shapiro Way
So. El Monte, CA 91733
*Chenille Chair p. 28(l),
Chenille Bunny p. 36(ur)*

Daisy Dimples
23705 Vanowen Street, Ste 157
West Hills, CA 91307
rubin818@yahoo.com
Picture Frames p. 36(ur), Picture Frames p. 41(u), Picture Frames p. 41(b)

Diana Dunkley
Chapelle Ltd.
204 25th Street
Ogden, UT 84401
www.chapelle@chapelleltd.com
p. 101

Downtown Company, Inc.
Fifty-Five Haul Road
Wayne, NJ 07470-6675
Blanket p. 31(r)

Elements
343 Main Street
Great Barrington, MA 01230
Photo Album p. 41(u)

Fun Bath
1734 East 12th Street
Oakland, CA 94606
Bath Robe, Hooded Towel, Bib p. 27(bl)

Gratitude & Co., Inc.
381 Main Street
Aurora, NY 13026
www.giftsofgratitude.com
Photo Box p. 41(u)

Grace Taormina
Rubber Stampede
967 Stanford Avenue
Oakland, CA 94608
Animal-print Floorcloth p. 123

Jan Sevadjian
11837 Judd Court #124
Dallas, TX 75243
jan@jansevadjian.com
Photo Albums p. 41(u)

Kerri Lee
1155 Nevada Avenue
San Jose, CA 95125
Blocks p. 33(ul), Stepping Stool p. 33(br), Door Sign p.22(b)

Lazertran LLC (USA)
650 8th Avenue
New Hyde Park, NY 11040
www.lazertran.com
Vintage Window p.19

Little Giraffe
17638 Sherman Way
Van Nuys, CA 91406
Burp Cloth p. 25(l), Blankets p. 26(ul), Baby Clothes p.22(u)

Petunia Pickle Bottom
416 Montgomery Street
Santa Barbara, CA 93103
www.petuniapicklebottom.com
Blanket p. 26(br)

Roman, Inc.
555 Lawrence Avenue
Roselle, IL 60172-1599
Ceramic Treasure Box p. 41(u)

Ruby & Begonia
204 Historic 25th Street
Ogden, Utah 84401
Milk Bottle p. 33(ur)

Sweet Tulip
42 West 72nd Street, 12B
New York, NY 10023
www.sweettulip.com
Baby Cup p. 36(ur), p. 41(b)

The Lorilyn Collection
1935 Palmer Avenue
Larchmont, NY 10538
www.lorilyn.com
Hanky Blankets p. 74(u), 75

Tobi Klein
24 Windsor Street
Arlington, MA 02474
Picture Pocket p. 33(ur)

Wild Wings / Dave Vissat
1122 Lincoln Way
White Oak, PA 15131
Birdhouse p. 32(ul)

Photography

**Kevin Dilley / Hazen Photography
Jill Dahlberg / Stylist**
5(u)(b), 9(ul), 10(u)(b), 12(u)(b), 13(l), 18(ul)(bl)(r), 19, 21, 22(u)(b), 23, 24, 25, 26, 27(l)(br), 28, 29, 30, 31(r), 32, 33, 36(ur), 37(u), 38(bl), 40, 41, 43(l), 51, 55(ur)(br), 56, 57, 63, 66, 67, 74, 75, 79(r), 80, 81, 82, 83, 84, 85, 92(b), 94, 101, 104(b), 105, 111, 112, 113, 114, 115, 116, 117, 118, 119, 121, 124(b), 125(u)

Jesse Walker
2, 3, 11(b), 13(ur), 16(uc)(r), 17(b), 27(ur), 35, 36(l)(br), 37(b), 39, 42, 43(r), 44, 45, 47, 48, 49, 50, 52, 54, 55(ul), 59, 60, 61, 62, 64, 65, 69, 70, 71, 72, 73, 76, 77, 78, 79(l), 87, 89(u), 90, 91, 97, 98, 99, 100, 102, 103, 104(u), 107, 108, 109, 110(u), 120, 121, 122, 124(u), 125(b)

Scot Zimmerman
11(r), 13(br), 14, 15(u)

Caroll McKanna Shreeve
illustrations 15(r)(b), 17, 29(ul)(lr), 38, 45, 62, 74, 77, 81, 88, 90, 93, 95, 100, 109, 120, 121

Digital Stock
110(b)

Corbis
89(b), 92(u)

Photodisc
8, 9(br), 31(l), 38(r)

David and Linda Durbano
111(ll), 112(ul), 113, 115(ul)

Kelly and Kathy Goddard
5(uc), 66, 67, 114(l)

Shane and Sue Walton
80, 81(l)(r), 82, 83(u)(l)

Timothy and Sue Houden
116, 117(ul)(lr), 118, 119

About the Author

Carol Scheffler is widely recognized in every form of media as a leading expert in crafting and life-style arts.

Carol is a featured contributor on morning news and talk shows such as the Today Show and the Rosie O'Donnell Show. She is also a regular guest on popular life-style shows on HGTV, Discovery Channel, PBS, and CNN.

Carol is a noted book author as well. Her latest books include *Crafting Fun Stuff with a Crowd of Kids*, *Family Crafting*, and *Rubber Stamping for the First Time*™.

Carol is proud to have served as the Hobby Industry Association's Spokesperson for National Craft Month, and the celebrity expert on Joann.com, the leading crafts and home design web site. She also serves as a crafting and life-styles authority on IVillage.com.

A frequent contributor to many magazines, Carol's designs can be found in *Parents Magazine*, *McCall's*, *Better Homes and Gardens*, *Creative Home*, *Popular Photography*, and *The Rubber Stamper*.

Dedication: This book is dedicated to the memory of my Mom, who taught me what "home" is really all about.

Thanks from the bottom of my heart to . . .

Jo Packham and Karla Haberstich of Chapelle, Ltd., whose patient, calm, and encouraging ways make each and every publishing experience with them warm and wonderful;

Grace Taormina, Rubber Stampede, and Delta Technical Coatings for their beautiful stamps, paints, and innovation;

And, of course, my family— Michael, Madeline, Eliza, and Susannah—who make "home" my favorite place to be.

Metric Equivalency Chart

		mm-millimetres		cm-centimetres	
		inches to millimetres and centimetres			
inches	mm	cm	inches	cm	inches	cm
---	---	---	---	---	---	---
1/8	3	0.3	9	22.9	30	76.2
1/4	6	0.6	10	25.4	31	78.7
3/8	10	1.0	11	27.9	32	81.3
1/2	13	1.3	12	30.5	33	83.8
5/8	16	1.6	13	33.0	34	86.4
3/4	19	1.9	14	35.6	35	88.9
7/8	22	2.2	15	38.1	36	91.4
1	25	2.5	16	40.6	37	94.0
1 1/4	32	3.2	17	43.2	38	96.5
1 1/2	38	3.8	18	45.7	39	99.1
1 3/4	44	4.4	19	48.3	40	101.6
2	51	5.1	20	50.8	41	104.1
2 1/2	64	6.4	21	53.3	42	106.7
3	76	7.6	22	55.9	43	109.2
3 1/2	89	8.9	23	58.4	44	111.8
4	102	10.2	24	61.0	45	114.3
4 1/2	114	11.4	25	63.5	46	116.8
5	127	12.7	26	66.0	47	119.4
6	152	15.2	27	68.6	48	121.9
7	178	17.8	28	71.1	49	124.5
8	203	20.3	29	73.7	50	127.0

Index